# PIONEERS OF
# RELIGIOUS EDUCATION

# PIONEERS OF
# RELIGIOUS EDUCATION

BY

T. F. KINLOCH

WITH A FOREWORD
BY
J. S. WHALE, D.D.

*Essay Index Reprint Series*

 BOOKS FOR LIBRARIES PRESS
FREEPORT, NEW YORK

First published 1939
Reprinted 1969

LIBRARY OF CONGRESS CATALOG CARD NUMBER:.

69-18929

MANUFACTURED
BY
HALLMARK LITHOGRAPHERS, INC.
IN THE U.S.A.

# FOREWORD

THIS book has an importance out of all proportion to its size, as parents, teachers and all who feel the urgency of the problem of Christian education in these times will realize. Its merits are many and obvious. Mr. Kinloch combines the learned research of the historian with the vitality and vigour of the experienced teacher who knows what he is talking about because he has tested it in practice. His book is a miracle of compression, presenting in a clear and comprehensive way a good deal of material not otherwise available in English. Perhaps his most valuable contribution to the problem of modern religious education is his virtual contention that the problem has not yet been solved.

Mr. Kinloch uses history to show us what the problem is. (1) Humanism demands that the Bible be properly interpreted. (2) The method of Catechism is an attempt to get the Bible properly understood. (3) The Jesuits show the importance of getting the emotions and the will properly trained. (4) Comenius reminds us that all knowledge is not confined to the ancients. (5) The very important chapter on Pietism and on Francke illustrates the difficulty of combining sound learning with true religion, and of introducing a definitely religious atmosphere into the school. (6) Pestalozzi's method is the right one, but (7) without Schleiermacher's great reminder that religion is an end in itself, even right methods will fail of their ultimate object.

v

The space at Mr. Kinloch's disposal for discussing the English aspect of this problem is tantalisingly small, yet he says enough about Arnold and the modern elementary school to make us see that the modern secondary school is the real problem. And yet the real problem is the Home and the Church, if those who teach are not to be burdened with an impossible task. If it be true that Christendom, menaced by gigantic secular forces, must think seriously about its future, this book is a good omen not only for the schools of our country but for the world at large.

J. S. WHALE

Cheshunt College
  Cambridge

# CONTENTS

# CHAPTER I

## *Introduction*

EVERY trained teacher knows that hundreds of books have been written to explain the theory of education ; that numerous manuals have been produced to show how such theory may be best applied. Yet, when asked to give religious instruction in a modern school, he soon discovers that few of the books he read at college afford assistance, or throw light on his two-fold problem : What *is* religious education ? What special technique, if any, does this particular subject require ?

The present volume is offered as a contribution to the solution of this difficult yet urgent problem ; and to avoid all risk of disappointment it is well to indicate the lines along which it proceeds.

A book on religious education may deal with the subject from one or other of two points of view. It may be a history from which the reader can learn how religious teaching was given in the past. It may recount the achievements and point out the failures of former teachers, and in so doing suggest the mistakes which their successors should avoid, the methods they may most profitably pursue. Or it may be a dogmatic treatise in which the writer expounds his own theory of religious education and indicates the way in which this theory may be most successfully applied. The present volume is neither. It is not a history of religious education ; nor is it an exposition of any particular theory. It is not a history of religious education for the simple reason that no single volume could afford sufficient scope for adequate treatment of so great a subject. The bulky volumes in which the older German writers on what they termed ' The History of Catechetical Instruction ' set forth their views are ample evidence of the amount of ground that has to be covered. In the present work, for instance, no reference is made to the ancient Hebrews, though it has been said that the Book of Proverbs is ' the oldest handbook of education ', and though it is certainly true that the Hebrew contribution to the theory of religious education is so important that it deserves, as it has received, a volume to itself.[1] No reference is made to the religious teaching given in the early Church, either in the days when most converts were adults, or in later times when most Christians, entering the Church through the door of infant baptism, received instruction before they were admitted to their first communion.

Nothing is said of the work done in the great ' Catechetical Schools ' of Alexandria. Nor is any but casual reference made to medieval schools, though Mr. Arthur F. Leach[2] has shown how numerous and varied they were, and though Maskell[3] maintains that ' It may very reasonably be said, that, taking the relative population of England in the years 1350 and 1750, there were more people who could read 200 years before the Reformation than 200 years afterwards.'

[1] Gollancz (Sir H.) : *Pedagogics of the Talmud and that of Modern Times : a comparative Study.* (Oxford Univ. Press, 1924.)
[2] A. F. Leach : *The Schools of Medieval England.*
[3] W. Maskell : *Monumenta Ritualia Ecclesiae Anglicanae,* III, 51.

To one feature of medieval education, however, we must call attention.

In Chaucer's Prioress's. Tale (l.72) we read

> This litel child his litel book lerninge,
> As he sat in the scole at his *prymer*.

The word Primer is used in a two-fold sense. From a liturgical point of view it was the People's Prayer Book, a collection of devotional material which gradually grew up to supplement the Divine Office. It varied from country to country, and indeed from place to place ; but it always included certain unvarying elements. After the breach with Rome in 1533 the English Primer assumed a much more Protestant tone. In 1545 it appeared in English : revised editions of this English Primer were issued by Elizabeth in 1560 and 1566.

The other sense in which the term is used is that of an elementary book on the cardinal points of Christian belief. It contained, before the breach with Rome, the ' invariable elements ' of the ' liturgical Primer ' which were preceded by the Alphabet, the Lord's Prayer, the Ave Maria, the Creed ; and this compilation was used as a first reading book. Hence, as some think, its name. In its more Protestant form the Primer was used in many schools, though by no means in all, from 1545 to 1651.

In medieval education the Primer played an important part. Teachers were, usually, monks or priests ; their pupils boys destined to become ' clercs '. The whole aim of education was avowedly religious. Even therefore if we did not know how deeply St. Paul's School was affected by medieval ideals, we could imagine that generations of schoolmasters had learnt something which was likely to prove of value to their successors. The medieval schoolmaster realized more clearly for instance than did some of those who followed him, that religious teaching demands a devotional atmosphere and that one of the greatest Christian virtues is humility.

At the same time it must be borne in mind that most medieval teaching was confined to those who were intended to become 'clercs'; that Schaff expresses the view of many if not of most scholars when he says, 'Upon the whole this duty (viz. that of imparting religious instruction) was sadly neglected in the Middle Ages and the people were allowed to grow up in ignorance and superstition';[1] that Erasmus, who was educated in one of the best monastic schools of his time, was never weary of denouncing the education given in such institutions, and went indeed so far as to say on more than one occasion that he preferred that there should be no school at all rather than one controlled by monks, *Scola sit publica aut nulla.*[2]

Unless, then, this work were to be expanded into several volumes, it is obvious that it could give no adequate account of Religious Education as we meet with it in the ancient world, the early Church, the Middle Ages. It deals with a mere fragment of an immense subject and begins with the Renaissance.

In the second place this book makes no pretension to be a systematic treatise on religious education. It is very doubtful if the time is ripe for such a work There is as yet too little agreement in regard to the scope and

[1] Schaff: *History of the Creeds*, I, 246.
[2] Erasmus: *De Pueris*, 504 C.I.

purpose of religious teaching in schools, and far too
little knowledge of religious psychology. At best, such
a book to-day can only be a pious expression of
individual opinion. None the less a beginning must be
made. In many Training Colleges students have
read ' How Gertrude teaches her children ', and thus
have learnt how much more interesting lectures on
Pestalozzi become when one begins by reading a
little of what Pestalozzi actually wrote. There is
something in the way in which a great master handles
any subject which no commentator, however skilled,
no lectures, however lucid, can reproduce.

> to watch
> The master work, and catch
> Hints of the proper craft, tricks of the tool's true play.

That is exactly what we propose to do.

In this book we shall watch the Masters at work to
see if we can learn from them the way in which they
dealt with their problems, and how we in turn should
handle ours. Nor will any teacher who remembers how
much is owed to Froebel, Herbart, Pestalozzi and
Rousseau be surprised to learn that some of the most
valuable contributions to a theory of religious education
have come to us from countries other than our own.

# CHAPTER II

## *Christian Humanism*

IT is obvious, even to the most casual observer, that certain mechanical inventions have altered the whole course of human life. The coming of the steam engine, the aeroplane, wireless, has changed the world. In the same way certain great spiritual movements have affected everyone. None can foretell the ultimate outcome of the Russian Revolution ; though we can measure, to some extent, the influence which the French Revolution exerted on the history of Europe and America. In the fifteenth century men felt that the change which came over Europe when the Middle Ages were left behind and the modern world began, was so profound that they called it the *Renaissance, the New Birth* : and some have sought to explain the change by saying that it was the birth of *Humanism*.

' Humanism ', it has been said, ' is a movement of the human mind which began with the rise of the towns when the urban intelligentsia slowly turned away from the transcendental values imposed by religion to the more immediately perceptible values of nature and man.' Its earliest beginnings are to be met with in the twelfth and thirteenth centuries : it ' arrived at consciousness of itself in the fourteenth century . . . and has steadily widened its empire ever since '.[1]

During the Middle Ages men held in theory, even if they did not always carry their theory into practice,

[1] F. Schevill : *History of Florence*, 317-18.

that life on earth is but a preparation for the life to come. Here man is but a pilgrim and stranger, he has no enduring city, he seeks one which is to come. For answer to such questions as to how this world came into being, how man's short life on earth is to be spent, they turned to priests and to the sacred writings from which theologians claimed to derive most of the knowledge they possessed.

With the coming of the modern world men no longer regarded religious teachers as the sole repositories of wisdom. They learned to look at the physical world through their own eyes, and formed their own opinions in regard to its nature and origin ; just as, when they asked themselves how best to live on earth they no longer assumed that the only adequate answer was given either by the Bible or by the teaching of the Church.

The Renaissance began in Italy and the form which it first assumed was determined by one of the greatest of Italians. The Revival of Learning, which dates from the fourteenth century, was led by Petrarch. It was essentially the rediscovery of the art and literature of ancient Rome ; a little later of the yet greater art and literature of ancient Greece.

Petrarch was a Christian, and there were great teachers, like Vittorino, who tried to reconcile the New Learning with the Christian faith ; yet, for the most part, as the movement developed and spread in Italy, the spirit of paganism gradually prevailed. The old Christian ideal of humility gave place to the new ideal of *Virtù*. Men had a passionate desire for *self*-development, for fame ; strove to make others envy *their* achievements, thrust their own personality into the

foreground, as was the way with the humanist ' orator '
—the very embodiment of Renaissance culture. Those
who went farthest in their admiration of antiquity and
sought to revive the antique world in Italy at the
expense of the Church, and the various forms of
government which then obtained, were unable to
realize their dreams. Popes and princes saw to that.
Yet though the Italian Renaissance had little effect on
the form of religion it inflicted grievous injury upon its
spirit. Many ecclesiastics, including certain of the
Popes, paid no attention to the moral precepts of the
Christian religion ; men like Cellini had little use for
Christian ethics ; political thinkers like Macchiavelli
found no place in their systems for the Sermon on the
Mount.

Thanks to the munificent patronage of families like
the Medici and certain Popes, manuscripts were
collected, libraries founded, scholars supported, and
some of the world's most famous pictures and sculpture
produced. Yet none of these things led to the much
needed reform in private and public morals : and the
very Popes who did most to encourage art and letters
did least to reform the Church. For neither did they
make any attempt to curb the worldly ambition, the
avarice, the profligacy for which many great ecclesiastics were notorious, nor did they seek to cure the
ignorance and superstition which was rife in the
ranks of the lower clergy. The Italian Renaissance did
much to enrich the life of the prosperous citizen; it did
little to alleviate the hard lot of the common people.
It was essentially aristocratic and concerned itself more
with artistic than with moral goodness. Yet it did
teach men to appreciate beauty and to admire the

noblest literature the world contained. It inspired them with a passionate desire for knowledge, taught them to go back to the sources, filled them with unwearied determination to learn what great writers of the past had actually written, taught them to spare no pains to discover the exact meaning of the manuscripts which ancient writers had left behind. This, as we shall soon see, was nothing less than a revolution. It changed man's entire attitude not only to the Classics but to the Bible. It is one of the most precious legacies the Italian Renaissance bequeathed.

The Renaissance reached Western Europe a hundred years after it appeared in Italy. By that time it had shed many of its youthful extravagances ; and from the outset it assumed a very different form in England and Germany from that which it had worn in Italy. In Italy, for instance, its effect on religion—save in the form of corroding scepticism—was slight ; in England and Germany it was profound. At first the New Learning and the Reforming movement were closely allied in Germany : in England a new attitude to Scripture was introduced which continues to this day. In England Humanism and Christianity were blended in a way to which Italy was an utter stranger. In England and Germany a new phenomenon appears. It is Christian Humanism.

# A

## DESIDERIUS ERASMUS (1466-1536)

Of all Christian Humanists Erasmus is perhaps the greatest as he is certainly the most widely known.

Born in Rotterdam in 1466 or 1467, educated in a monastic school, he appears in Oxford in 1498. There he meets Colet and, under Colet's influence, resolves to dedicate his life to the study and exposition of religion. With this in view he goes to Paris where he studies Greek. From 1506 to 1509 he is in Italy : from 1510 to 1513 he is in Cambridge, where he lectures on Greek and is Lady Margaret professor of Divinity. In 1516 he publishes his edition of the Greek Testament—the first ever issued. From 1516 to 1536 he is in Basel, where he dies.

Within the narrow limits of this book it is impossible to trace the change which came over Erasmus as he turned from the views of the monks by whom he was educated to the New Learning of which he became the best known and most brilliant advocate. That has been done by Otto Schottenloher.[1] Nor is there need for a detailed account of his educational writings. That has been done once for all by W. H. Woodward in a brilliant monograph.[2] We shall content ourselves with giving a brief account of the views he held after Colet had laid his hand upon him.

From the first he was opposed to the barbarous Latin used by the monks, and insisted that a knowledge of Latin should be acquired through study of the Classics. He did this not merely on aesthetic grounds, but because he was persuaded, like every humanist, that classical literature contained the sum and substance of all human knowledge. Knowledge of the content of the

[1] O. Schottenloher : *Erasmus im Ringen um die humanistische Bildungswesen* (1933).
[2] W. H. Woodward : *Desiderius Erasmus concerning the method of Education.*

classics as well as of their form was essential therefore
to every educated man. In the second place, he was
convinced that religious truth could not be reached
through scholasticism and the dialectical method with
which it was combined. To him it seemed sheer waste
of time to discuss how many angels could balance
themselves on the point of a needle—to take an extreme
instance of dialectical futility ;   the only study of
religion of any value was the text of Scripture and the
writings of the earliest Fathers. It was all the easier
for Erasmus to adopt this attitude because by nature
and temperament he was incapable of taking any
interest in metaphysics. Metaphysic and the theology
that was based upon it meant almost nothing to him :
religious ceremonies of any kind meant little more.
For him the simple practical teaching contained in the
Gospels was the sum and substance of religious knowledge :   Christ's earthly life the perfect example of
moral purity and goodness. Man's happiness lay in
trying to follow in the Master's footsteps. That was
theology enough.   Hence he longed for the day when
simple folk would be able to read the Bible in their own
mother tongue.  ' I long ', he said, ' that the husband-
man should sing them (i.e. the Scriptures) to himself
as he follows the plough, that the weaver should hum
them to the tune of his shuttle, that the traveller should
beguile with them the weariness of his journey.' It has
been often said that Erasmus was not one of the
' twice-born '. Of the spiritual struggles of such men as
St. Paul and Luther he knew almost nothing, just as he
had no experience of the mysticism, the heavenly
rapture which we meet with in the lives of the greatest
saints. The ' World of Antiquity ' of which he spoke

was not the real antique world with all its sin and
tragedy. It was a world bathed in light which never
was on land or sea. From this world, purged of
intractable elements, he selected that which was most
in harmony with Christian thought and feeling;
from the Christian religion, released from its more
mystical and speculative aspects, he took certain
other elements, and fused them into one. This was
Christian humanism as Erasmus understood it ;
and nearly every other Christian humanist followed
in his steps.

Like the ancient Greeks, Erasmus was too apt to
identify virtue with knowledge, to assume that if man
only knew the good he was bound to do it. He did not
always realize that certain devils are only driven out
' with prayer and fasting '. Yet despite his short-
comings his influence on Religious Education was
profound. In contrast to Italian humanists he taught
that the end of all education was to train boys to serve
God and their fellow men. To Erasmus ignorance was
the mortal foe of genuine religion. The most perfect
form of Christianity was that which combined simple
faith in Christ and readiness to serve Him, with ample
knowledge of every form of excellence which the best
of men had revealed in literature and in life. No one
believed more firmly in the Apostle's words or did
more, according to the measure of his strength to carry
them out in practice : ' whatsoever things are true,
whatsoever things are honourable, whatsoever things
are just, whatsoever things are pure, whatsoever things
are lovely, whatsoever things are of good report ; if
there be any virtue, and if there be any praise, think on
these things.'

B

## JOHN COLET (1467?-1519)

Colet was born in London, of which his wealthy
father was twice Lord Mayor. He went to Oxford,
thence to Paris, and thereafter to Italy to study canon
and civil law and the elements of Greek. In his travels
he became imbued with the spirit of the New Learning,
met Erasmus, and, as some say, heard Savonarola
preach. On his return to England he took orders and
settled down in Oxford. Though not a Doctor of
Divinity he delivered lectures on the Epistles of St.
Paul. These lectures aroused great attention and were
attended by every person of note in the University.
They were entirely different from any lectures that had
been heard before in Oxford ; for Colet abandoned
the scholastic method and gave a simple exposition of
the meaning of the text. These lectures therefore mark
a turning point in the history of religious education
in England.

In 1498 Erasmus came to Oxford and formed an
intimate friendship with Colet, who persuaded him to
make the study and exposition of the Scriptures his
life work. He also persuaded him that the methods of
the New Learning not only could but should be applied
to the interpretation of Scripture.

In 1505 Colet became Dean of St. Paul's and continued to lecture on the Books of the Bible. In 1508 his
father died and he became possessed of a large fortune.
With this he built and endowed St. Paul's School, the
first humanistic school to be established in England.
He placed it in the care of the Mercers' Company, and
thus it was the first school to be managed by laymen.

Colet made William Lilly, the celebrated Grammarian who had studied Greek in Rhodes, his first High Master.

In the ' Statutes ' Colet explains that his chief purpose in founding St. Paul's was ' to increase knowlege and worshipping of god and oure lorde Crist Jesu and good Cristen lyff and maners in the children '. To this end he ordains that boys shall begin by learning the *Cathechyzon* in English. The contents of the *Cathechyzon* are as follows : (1) The Apostles' Creed, (2) The seven sacraments, (3) A brief explanation of Charity, (4) Emphasis is laid on the need of (*a*) Penance, (*b*) Holy Communion (Howselinge), (*c*) Extreme Unction, (5) Then follow fifty short precepts such as ' Fear God : Love God : Bridal the affections of thy mind : Believe and trust in Christ Jesu : Worship him and his mother Mary : Use ofttime Confession : Love all men in God.' ' By this way ', he concludes, ' thou shalt come to grace and glory.' The book ends with three additional pieces which are printed in Latin, (*a*) The Apostles' Creed, (*b*) The Lord's Prayer, (*c*) The Angel's Salutation, and two Latin prayers.

Thus, then, though Colet was a fearless critic of evils in the Church, and though he was wholeheartedly in favour of the New Learning, he was not a Protestant. As we pointed out in our first chapter the religious teaching given in St. Paul's was strongly affected by medieval devotion. In one respect, however, he was nearer in spirit to the English Grammar schools, with which we shall deal in the next chapter, than he was to either Erasmus or Melancthon—the Preceptor of Germany—or to Sturm, the greatest exponent of

Christian Humanism in the German Schools. He regarded the Classics with suspicion.

In his commentary on 1st Corinthians he says :

> If we seek to feed on the wisdom of the heathen, which is devilish, not Christian, we lose the principles of our Lord. . . . Those books in which Christ is not found are but a table of devils. Do not become readers of philosophers, companions of devils.
>
> In the choice and well-stored table of Holy Scripture all things are contained that belong to the truth.[1]

Colet was a wise man and did not tie down St. Paul's to his own views. But the Latin authors which he recommended for reading in school are not classical. Whilst he believed that the ideal mental discipline is that provided by the study of Greek and Latin, he believed no less firmly that any rule of life which is worth following is to be found in Scripture.

We must now consider the difference between the interpretation of Scripture which obtained in the medieval church and that which was introduced through the Revival of Learning. We have already described it as revolutionary.

When the medieval student read a passage of Scripture he sought to find in it four different meanings. He interpreted it in *four* different ways which he termed (*a*) literal or historical, (*b*) allegorical, (*c*) moral or tropological, (*d*) anagogical. ' In some cases ', says Dr. Lupton, ' it was held that an expression might be interpreted in all four ways: For instance, "waters" in Gen. i. 9, " Let the waters under the heaven," etc., was in its literal sense. In Isaiah xliii. 2, " When thou

---

[1] Colet on 1st Cor., Lupton's Trans., p. 110.

passest through the waters, I will be with thee," it was in the moral sense. In Ezekiel xxxvi. 25, " Then will I sprinkle clean water upon you," it was in the allegorical sense, being understood of baptism. And lastly in Jeremiah ii. 13, " They have forsaken me the fountain of living waters," it was in the anagogical, or elevating sense, by which, that is to say, our thoughts are raised from the earthly to the heavenly."[1]

Perhaps the best way in which to understand the matter is to turn to Neale's *Commentary on the Psalms.* Neale was saturated in the spirit of medievalism, and had an immense knowledge of medieval writing. In these volumes he collects comments on the Psalter from great medieval divines. Let us turn for example to the eighth psalm and let us take the eighth verse :

> The fowl of the air, and the fish of the sea, and whatsoever passeth through the paths of the seas.

This is how medieval commentators interpreted it :

> The *fowls of the air* are the saints who rise above the world, but only by means of the sign of the cross. The *fishes*, ordinary Christians, regenerate of water and of the Holy Ghost : *and whatsoever*, bad as well as good, unholy no less than holy, *walketh through the paths of the seas*, is exposed to the waves and storms of this troublesome world. Augustine, however, says that *the fowls of the air* are the proud and ambitious, the fishes those who are restless and acquisitive. Others again maintain that the *winged fowls* are the angels ; the *fishes* the evil spirits of the abyss. Others again that the *fish* are the dwellers in the isles afar off, and mariners in them, who walk through the paths of the seas.

[1] *Life of Colet,* p. 105.

In his 3rd Dissertation on *The mystical and literal interpretation of the Psalms* Neale quotes with disapproval a passage from Dr. Scott, a well-known commentator of the day :

> At this rate, you may prove any doctrine from any text ; everything is reduced to uncertainty, as if the Scripture had no determinate meaning, till one was arbitrarily imposed by the imagination of men.

After having condemned the ' mystical ' interpretation in vigorous terms, William Tyndale says :

> Thou shalt understand that the scripture hath but one sense, which is the literal sense. And that literal sense is the root and ground of all, and the anchor that never faileth, whereunto if thou cleave, thou canst never err or go out of the way. And if thou leave the literal sense thou canst not but go out of the way.[1]

On the allegorical or mystical interpretation of Scripture some most important doctrines were based. For instance, in the Bull *Unam Sanctam* of Boniface VIII (1302) we read :

> By the words of the gospel we are taught that the two swords, namely, the spiritual authority and the temporal are in the power of the church. For when the apostles said ' Here are two swords ' (Luke xxii. 38)—that is, in the church, since it was the apostles who were speaking—the Lord did not answer, ' It is too much', but ' It is enough'. Whoever denies that the temporal sword is in the power of Peter does not properly understand the word of the Lord when he said : ' Put up thy sword into the sheath ' (John xviii. 11).

---

[1] *Doctrinal Treatises* (Parker Society), p. 304.

> Both swords, therefore, the spiritual and the temporal, are in the power of the church.[1]

Even Erasmus found it very hard to abandon the old method of interpretation and to embrace the new. On one occasion he said that we might as well read the story of Livy as the Book of Judges, or many other parts of the Old Testament, if we left out of account their allegorical meaning. But for the most part he remained true to the new method as did all the humanists.

> In the writings of the New Testament [said Colet], saving when it pleased the Lord Jesus and His Apostles to speak in parables as Christ often does in the Gospels, and St. John throughout in the Revelation, all the rest of the discourse, in which either the Saviour teaches His disciples more plainly, or the Apostles instruct the Churches, has the sense that appears on the surface ; nor is one thing said and another meant, but the very thing is meant which is said, and the sense is wholly literal.

This, then, was the great change in the interpretation of Scripture, which the Renaissance introduced. Men no longer approached the Scriptures with ready made ideas which they read into the sacred text in the most arbitrary manner ; they went to the Scriptures to discover, by patient study, what they had to teach. Calvin, the greatest of Protestant commentators, was able on his death bed to say that he had never read his own fancies into Scripture, but had tried throughout his life to discover, with the help of God, what Scripture had to teach.

The first task, then, for the Christian humanist was

[1] Thatcher and McNeil : *A Source Book for Medieval History*, p. 315.

to obtain as correct a version as he could of the sacred text ; his next to interpret the text in the most simple and natural way. For him the principles by which Christians had to guide their lives were contained in the New Testament : yet these principles did not conflict with anything good or true or beautiful which gifted heathens had discovered. Christ is not the enemy of truth or beauty. He came into the world to enrich, not to narrow, human life. In His religion, as in the *pietas literata*, which the humanist schoolmaster sought to produce, there is room for every noble thought that has as yet entered the mind of man.

' To humanism ', says a recent writer, ' we owe our modern respect for veracity and our modern distrust of abstract speculation divorced from fact.' To Christian humanism, we may add, we owe the desire to make use of every means that God has given to assist us in our search for truth and the conviction that a cultured gentleman who devotes his life to the service of his fellows and the State is the most perfect embodiment of the Christian character.

# CHAPTER III

## *The English Grammar School (1558-1660)*

CHRISTIAN Humanism, so brilliantly advocated by Erasmus, so nobly embodied in Colet, never gained a footing in England : its doom was sealed by the Reformation. To learn the nature of the religious teaching given in this country between the accession of Elizabeth and the Restoration we must turn to Mr. Foster Watson. His brilliant book, *The English Grammar School to 1660*—a veritable mine of wealth on all that concerns English education during this period—is not likely to be superseded for many years to come.

Luther was excommunicated in 1520. From that time forward right on to the beginning of the eighteenth century, when men, having grown weary of theological argument, turned to rationalism, all Europe was involved and was intensely interested in theological dispute. The discussion was by no means of a calm academic order ; it was war to the death. To realize this we have but to recall the Marian persecution in England, the 'Bloody Council' of Alva who boasted that he had executed 18,000 men in the Netherlands, the Massacre of St. Bartholomew, the Spanish Armada, the Gunpowder Plot; to recall, too, the Thirty Years' War which devastated Germany, the eight 'Wars of Religion' in France, the Revocation of the Edict of Nantes in 1685, when a quarter of a million of the most industrious and virtuous Frenchmen were forced to flee the country. ' The French ', said Voltaire, ' were as widely dispersed as the Jews.'

It is safe to say that there has never been a quarrel about religion which was simply and solely concerned with religion. The Reformation in England, as in Germany, was largely affected by political considerations. The same holds good of the Thirty Years' War and of the ' Wars of Religion ' in France. Nevertheless the fact remains that for more than a hundred and fifty years Europe was divided into two hostile camps and that the banners under which they were arrayed bore religious emblems. In those days men were as keenly interested in theological questions as the modern man is in economic questions : the conflicting ideals of Catholic and Protestant had then the same importance, the same practical interest, as the opposing political principles of the Authoritarian and Democratic States have to-day. Then religion was felt to be the one question of *absolute* importance : Catholic and Protestant in fighting with each other were convinced that they were maintaining the cause of God. We can only understand the importance attached to the study of Catechism and Bible in the religious education of the period if we bear in mind the background of intense conviction and bitter conflict to which we have referred.

The earliest Protestant influence came to England from Germany. Cranmer and many others were deeply affected by Luther ; but after the return of the Marian exiles Luther ceased to have much influence in England. His place was taken by Calvin. Indeed it is difficult to exaggerate the influence which Calvin exercised on English religious thought—and nowhere was his influence greater than in the school—between 1558 and 1660.

The essence of Calvin's view of religious education is clearly stated in the sixth of the XXXIX Articles :

> Holy Scripture containeth all things necessary to salvation : so that whatsoever is not read therein, nor may be proved thereby, is not to be required of any man, that it should be believed as an article of the Faith, or be thought requisite and necessary to salvation.

Calvin maintained that from the study of Scripture man learned all that he need know to live aright. All theories concerning the good life, whether met with in the writings of heathen philosophers, or contained in the traditions of the Church, had to be submitted to this test. Through the *Bible* God spoke to man ; man's chief end was to learn the will of God and to do it.

But the Bible is a big book. It contains many things, as Calvin, the most honest of commentators, was the first to admit, which are exceedingly difficult, sometimes impossible to understand. Therefore it was requisite that competent scholars, who had studied the Bible, should reduce the sum and substance of its teaching to a simple form which even the dullest and simplest could understand. Hence the Catechism, a book from which the young might learn those unspeakably precious truths for belief in which their fathers had suffered and fought and died ; a book by means of which the young might be so firmly grounded in the truth that no assault of the enemy, however subtle, could prevail upon them to abandon it.

So far we have spoken as if those who forsook the

old religion to embrace the new were in complete accord. That, however, was very far from being the case. All Protestants were agreed that Rome—the Scarlet Woman, as they often termed her—was their common foe : yet on the Continent in general, and in Germany in particular, Wittenberg and Geneva were constantly at war. In England many Puritans were opposed to the policy of the National Church. In 1655 Richard Baxter deplored the bitterness of party strife. ' We have ', he said, ' as sad divisions among us in England, considering the piety of the persons, and the smallness of the matter of our discord, as most nations under heaven have known.'

From the introduction which Professor Woodhouse has written to the volume entitled *Puritanism and Liberty*, which contains a record of the ' Army Debates ' (1647-9), one may learn how political principles were determined by religious convictions. Be that as it may, the point to remember is that throughout this whole period men took a passionate interest in religious questions, felt that everything depended on the acquisition, the maintenance, and the propagation of religious truth. Hence the zeal—perhaps unequalled before or since—with which they taught religion, perhaps one ought rather to say theology, in the school.

Never before or since have English schoolboys been taught so much theology, never have they spent so much time in learning the Catechism. That is the burden of this chapter ; to it we shall presently return. Meanwhile it is necessary to call attention to certain facts.

(1) Broadly speaking the school syllabus included two subjects : Classics and Religion. The first it owed

to the Renaissance, the second to the Reformation. Erasmus read the classics not only because he admired their style but also because he wished to learn the view of life which they express. The English schoolboy, like his master, read the ancient writers of Greece and Rome not to discover their opinions—with these he was not concerned—but to master their language. Until the eighteenth century university lectures in this as in other countries were given in Latin. A command of graceful Latin was as essential then to every man who sought to enter a profession as the possession of a School Certificate is now to those who aspire to be more than hewers of wood and drawers of water. It was Cicero's style, not his opinions, that was valued. The boy's view of life was determined by the Bible.

(2) Every boy who attended a Grammar School came from what is now called a ' religious ' home. Woodward says, ' At no time in modern history was care of, and interest in the young so striking a fact of society as in the Italy of the Quattrocento.' At no period, we may add, in modern history was so much attention given by parents to family worship as in the time of the Puritans.

> We have filled our children's bones with sin [says Hezekiah Woodward]. It is our engagement to do all we can to root that sin out, which we have been a means to root so fast in. We see what an engagement it is, *the greatest and strongest that can be thought of.*

(3) Watson gives many quotations from School statutes to show the emphasis laid on school worship. One, typical of so many others, must suffice. In the Harrow rules (1580) we read :

The first thing which shall be done in the morning, and the last in the evening before they depart, shall be upon their knees with reverence, to say Prayers, to be conceived by the Master and by one whom he shall appoint, distinctly to be pronounced, unto whom all the residue shall answer—Amen.

(4) It was part of the schoolmaster's duty to take his boys to church. The Statutes of Tonbridge School (circ. 1564) are typical :

Item, I will that all the scholars upon the Sabbath and holy days resort in due time to divine service in the parish church of Tunbridge, the Master or Usher or one of them at the least being present to oversee them. And I will that the master and usher do duely every Monday in the morning call to reckoning all such of the scholars as either absent themselves from the Church or come tarde to it or otherwise use not themselves reverently in prayer, every one of them having a Prayer book in Latin or English according to the Master's appointment.

In 1660 Charles Hoole published his *New Discovery of the Old Art of Teaching School*. From that interesting work we learn what was done in his time. On Sunday morning, an hour before Divine Service, the school assembled. The Master gave a lesson on the Catechism. After this a hymn was sung and a prayer was said. Then two by two the schoolboys marched to church. In the afternoon, after service, the boys return to school and the Master examines them on what they ' have heard or writ at the sermon '. Of the younger boys less was demanded ; the elder boys were expected to present full notes of the sermon.

In the seventeenth century men believed that if religious education were to be satisfactory it had to include, in addition to the training received at home and the instruction given in school, exposition by an expert ; exposition not merely to be heard and straightway forgotten, but impressed on the mind of the hearer in such a way that it would remain with him through life. Whatever the Puritan schoolboy knew or did not know, one lesson he was assuredly taught : knowledge of God is not acquired by those who are idle and listless ; it comes to those and to those alone who grudge no effort to obtain wisdom, who make their own the noble motto of G. F. Watts : ' the Utmost for the Highest.'

(5) For reasons already stated the Grammar School boy did not limit his Latin authors to the so-called Classics. Everybody then used Lilly's Latin Grammar. It begins with eighty-six Latin verses—*Carmen de Moribus*—an epitome of manners. From this poem the boy was supposed to learn his duties for the day ; to wash his face and hands, to keep his clothes clean, to comb his hair, and so forth. ' It is difficult to realize ', says Watson, ' that formerly these verses were probably as well known in England as any line of the Classics.'

But there was another and a much more famous way in which the boy was taught manners and morals. That was the Colloquy. The Colloquy was a book written in the form of a dialogue in which almost every conceivable subject was discussed. Its primary purpose was, of course, to teach a boy to speak correct Latin ; it had, however, another end in view. Through the Colloquy the boy was supposed to learn as much as possible of the world in which he would have to live, the people with whom he would come into contact, the way of life a Christian gentleman should seek to follow. It was at once a text-book of manners and of morals, and was based on the belief that, in the case of the young, general concepts like ' goodness ' are too vague for ethical instruction. Form must be filled with content ; ' goodness ' must be broken up into its constituent parts.

## THE CATECHISM

The earliest catechisms were produced by the Waldensians and the Bohemian Brethren. Interesting as they are to any student of cathechetics, they matter little to the general reader. It is otherwise with the work of one of the greatest men of religious genius the world has seen. Distressed at the ' lamentable state of religious ignorance and immorality amongst the German people ' Martin Luther produced a catechism in 1529. It consisted of five parts, and dealt with (1) The Decalogue, (2) The Apostles' Creed, (3) The Lord's Prayer, (4) Baptism, (5) The ' Sacrament of the Altar '. ' It exhibits ', says Schaff, ' his almost apostolic gift of expressing the deepest things in the plainest language for the common people. It is strong food for a man and yet as simple as a child. Luther himself wrote no better book, excepting, of course, his translation of the Bible, and it alone would have immortalized him as one of the great benefactors of the human race.'[1] The great historian, von Ranke, says of it : ' The Catechism published by Luther in 1529, of which he himself says that, old a doctor as he was, he used it himself as a prayer, is

[1] *History of the Creeds*, I, 250.

as childlike as it is profound, as comprehensible as it is unfathomable, simple and sublime. . . .'[1]

No other man has written such a catechism ; for no other man has equalled Luther in his marvellous power of expressing profound religious truths in simple vivid and popular speech. It has had an enormous influence in Germany ; it has had little influence in England. For until the Westminster Divines published their Shorter Catechism in 1647, two other catechisms were widely used : Calvin's Catechism (1538) and the Heidelberg Catechism (1563). Of the latter Schaff says, ' It is an acknowledged masterpiece with few to equal it and none to surpass it.' Even more widely used than either of these were two other catechisms : (1) The Catechism printed in the Book of Common Prayer. This was only used in the lower forms as it was regarded as containing the bare minimum of knowledge demanded of those who were confirmed. (2) In the upper forms, Nowell's Latin Catechism. To that important work we now must turn.

## NOWELL'S LATIN CATECHISM

Nowell was born in 1507 and became Dean of St. Paul's in 1560. Strype tells us that the catechism was finished in 1563 and that in 1570 the two Archbishops ' called upon the Dean to publish it '.[2] It was the official catechism of the Anglican Church and was used in the upper forms of almost every school throughout this period.

Nowell was equally admired as an exponent of

---

[1] *German History in the Time of the Reformation*, II, 3rd Ed. (1852).
[2] John Strype : *The Life and Acts of Archbishop Grindal*.

moderate Calvinism and as the possessor of an exceedingly graceful style. In the preface to his translation
of the catechism Thomas Norton says, ' in which
catechism there hath also great labour been bestowed
about the purity of the Latin tongue, that such as were
studious of that language, specially the youth, might
at once with one labour learn the truth of religion and
the pureness of the Latin tongue together '.

The catechism consists of about four hundred
questions and answers. Some of the answers (though by
no means all) are very lengthy. At times they extend to
two hundred words and it is difficult to believe that
any boy was capable of learning Nowell by heart.

The opening question and answer give some indica-
tion of the tone which pervades the book.

> *Master.* Forasmuch as the master ought to be to
> his scholars a second parent and father, not of their
> bodies, but of their minds, I see it belongeth to the
> order of my duty, my dear child, not so much to
> instruct thee civilly in learning and good manners, as
> to furnish thy mind, and that in thy tender years, with
> good opinions and true religion. For this age of child-
> hood ought no less, yea, also, much more, to be trained
> with good lessons to godliness, than with good arts to
> humanity : wherefore I thought meet to examine thee
> by certain short questions, that I may surely know
> whether thou have well bestowed thy study and
> labour therein, or no.
>
> *Scholar.* And I for my part, right worshipful master,
> shall willingly answer your demands, so far as I have
> heard you teach me out of the holy scriptures. (Norton's
> Trans.)

The boy, who professes to be a Christian, is then

asked what the Christian religion is. ' It is ', he replies,
' the true and godly worshipping of God and keeping
of his commandments.' It is to be learnt ' of none
other but of the heavenly word of God himself, which
he hath left unto us written in the holy scriptures '.
The whole of religion may be divided into four parts :
obedience, faith, invocation, and sacraments. If we
wish to know the sort of obedience which we have to
render we must turn to the Law.

> The Law of God [says the scholar] is the full and in
> all points perfect rule of the righteousness that is
> required of man, which commandeth those things that
> are to be done and forbiddeth the contraries. In this
> law God hath restrained all things to his own will and
> judgment, so as no godliness toward him, nor dutiful-
> ness toward men can be allowed of him, but that only
> which doth in all things agree with the straitness of
> this rule. Vainly, therefore, do mortal men invent to
> themselves forms of godliness and duty after their own
> fancy ; for God hath set forth to us his law, written
> in two tables, as a most sure rule both of our worship-
> ping of God, and of our duties to him, and therewith
> also hath declared that there is nothing on earth more
> pleasant and acceptable to him than our obedience.

After dealing at length with the Decalogue, Nowell
turns to the Apostles' Creed—the sum of faith. In this
section such weighty matters are handled, at considerable length, as the Fall of man who was created a
perfect being—the story of Genesis is understood in the
most literal way. ' The image of God in which man
was fashioned was ', says the scholar, ' most absolute
righteousness and most perfect holiness, which most
properly belongeth to the very nature of God, and

which hath been most evidently shewed in Christ our new Adam, and whereof in us there now scarcely appear any sparkles.' The Holy Trinity, original Sin, the Atonement, the Last Judgement, the Catholic Church (some sharp things are said of the presumptuous claims of the Bishop of Rome), the Resurrection of the flesh (carnis), the relation between Faith and Good Works, and many other points, are carefully discussed. Finally there is an exposition of the Lord's Prayer and of the Sacraments. So far as the present writer is able to judge the doctrine of the Eucharist which Nowell presents is almost identical with that of Calvin.

Such, then, was the catechetical instruction which, for more than a hundred years, a boy in the upper forms of an English Grammar school received. It was made possible by the fact that the curriculum was circumscribed, was confined almost entirely to Religion and the Classics and that long hours were spent on both.

It now remains to sum up as best we can the lessons that this period has to teach.

(1) In no period were men more firmly convinced that without the religious element as its controlling factor all education is inadequate. It is like *Hamlet* with Hamlet left out.

(2) They were equally confident that unless religious education is based on Holy Scripture it will be given in vain ; it will depend in the last resort upon an authority that is purely human and is ever changing. Scripture contains all that is essential : the catechism merely formulates the message of Scripture, it adds nothing to it.

(3) If the Bible is to be ' a lamp unto our feet, a

light unto our path ' it demands diligent study ; we must *search* the Scriptures. Home, school and Church must unite in continuous effort to impress on the child's mind those lessons which he must learn if he is to live aright.

(4) This is no place in which to discuss the use of a simple catechism.[1] Men differ even now in their estimate of its value. In regard to an elaborate catechism, such as Nowell's, there can be no two opinions. ' A young man ', it was once said, ' in the heat of his lust and passion, was judged to be no fit auditor of philosophy.' On the same principle a boy is hardly in a fit condition to profit by an elaborate and intricate exposition of the doctrine of the Atonement. In the sixteenth and seventeenth centuries schoolmasters were so eager to fill the minds of their pupils with important truths that they forgot the saying of the Wise Man, ' There is a time for all things.' A boy cannot learn too much great poetry when he is young. It will abide in his memory for ever and will as time goes on, and experience is widened, reveal its beauty and truth in ever richer measure. This, however, does not hold good of philosophical or theological formulae. Here form and content must advance *pari passu*. That is why no modern educationist would approve the use of Nowell's Catechism : for education means more than instruction. It is the development of the whole personality.

In that great age one of the greatest of Englishmen stated the aim of all education thus. ' It is ', says Milton, ' to repair the ruins of our first parents by regaining to know God aright, and out of that knowledge to love

[1] For the best short discussion of the subject, see J. L. Ewald : *Etwas ueber Catechismen.* (Heidelberg, 1816.)

him, to imitate him, to be like him, as we may the nearest by possessing our souls of true virtue, which being united to the heavenly grace of faith makes up the highest perfection.'

Every book on religious education must include some reference to Melancthon and Sturm.

(1) ' Wherever Luther prevails ', said Erasmus, ' the cause of literature and learning is lost.' The man who saved the situation was Melancthon (1497-1560), who became Professor of Greek at Wittenberg when twenty-one. ' Without the study of languages and philosophy', he said, 'the new doctrine cannot live and thrive.' He revived the universities and founded schools. His students called him *Praeceptor noster communis, praeceptor Germaniae.* In his own person he united as did no other the Renaissance and the Reformation. See Paulsen, op. cit., pp. 58-9.

(2) John Sturm (1507-89) was, perhaps the greatest of all humanistic schoolmasters, admired by Charles V, Ferdinand I, and Elizabeth. At one time in his school in Strassburg he had two hundred nobles, twenty-four counts and barons, with three princes. The Jesuits copied Sturm. His goal was to produce *sapiens atque eloquens pietas.* (See Paulsen, op. cit., 68, 195.) In his view *pietas* meant true doctrine ; *eloquentia* meant linguistic learning and *sapientia* the sciences (artes). In his old age (1581) he was deposed. His humanism was unpalatable to the dominant party on the City Council.

# CHAPTER IV

## *The Early Jesuits*

### IGNATIUS LOYOLA

LITTLE need be said here of Ignatius Loyola (1491-1556) who founded the Society of Jesus. A Spanish gentleman, he served first as page at the court of Ferdinand and Isabella, thereafter as a soldier. In 1521 he was wounded, and during a tedious convalescence, having exhausted his supply of romances, read the *Life of Christ* and the *Flowers of the Saints*. He was converted, went on a pilgrimage to Jerusalem, returned to Barcelona in 1524 where he began to learn Latin ; two years later he went to Alcala to study philosophy. At first his religious views were regarded with suspicion, especially at the University of Salamanca whither he had gone to study. But in 1528 he became a student at Paris (where he took his degree as Master) ; a year later he met the friends who became the first fathers of the Society of Jesus. In 1534 they met in the crypt of St. Mary's Church, Montmartre, and took the vows of poverty and chastity. They pledged themselves to go as missionaries to the Holy Land, or to tend the sick, or failing this to go to Rome and place themselves at the disposal of the Pope.

In 1537 Loyola became a priest, and said Mass for the first time in Santa Maria Maggiore (Rome) in 1538. A year later the ' Company of Jesus ' was formally constituted. Ignatius settled down in Rome. The Society prospered, and in 1547 Ignatius tried to resign the generalship of the order. The same thing happened in 1550. On each occasion, however, the fathers unanimously opposed the General's plan. In 1556 he did resign, and died suddenly in Rome on July 31st, 1556.

## THE SOCIETY OF JESUS

The ' Society of Jesus ' has had many enemies. At one time or another it has been expelled from almost every country in Europe. In 1773 it was dissolved by the Pope. Yet it still survives. As early as 1575 a Heidelberg professor published an oration in which he denounced ' the impious schools of the Jesuits and those who entrusted their sons to their care '. Borrowing a phrase from Virgil, he described the Society as ' monstrum horrendum ingens '. Pascal, one of the most gifted sons of a gifted race, directed the pointed shafts of his brilliant wit against the Society ; in the *Provincial Letters* he held up the moral teaching of the Jesuits to scorn and ridicule. On the other hand, men who had little sympathy with Jesuit views on religion and ethics admired their schools. In this Bacon and Descartes were at one ; great historians like von Ranke, great educationists like Paulsen, have paid tribute to their excellence. In one passage Paulsen says that for between 200 and 300 years the Jesuit schools were the best in Europe ; in another that in many respects their methods of instruction have never been surpassed. ' I am convinced ', he says, ' that the teachers whom the Order provided for the Roman Catholic countries were the best, the most learned, the most capable, and the most dutiful that could have been found for them.'[1]

[1] *German Education* (Eng. Trans.), p. 82.

To what, then, do they owe their excellence ? The answer is two-fold. 1. Loyola conceived a plan which he carried out with unwavering resolution. He knew exactly what he wanted to do and he did it. 2. The method which he designed, the system which he organized, were most admirably calculated to effect his purpose.

His purpose was to regain the territory which the Church of Rome had lost through the Reformation, and to do this by means of education. The motto of the Society was *Omnia ad maiorem Dei gloriam* ; its professed aim to ' teach the catechism to children and the ignorant, to instruct the young in Grammar Schools and Colleges '. ' Education ', says Paulsen, ' so largely prevails in the activity of the Order that it can be called in a special sense a *teaching* or *school* order.' Scholars who have studied the *Ratio Studiorum*[1] have tried to indicate the sources from which it is derived. 1. Undoubtedly much is due to the personal experience of Ignatius himself. No man strove harder than he to carry out the Socratic maxim, ' Know thyself '. He knew himself, and because he knew himself so well he knew human nature through and through. In this respect at least the Jesuits have never been excelled. 2. Like all other teachers of his age he was convinced that education should be based on a thorough knowledge of Latin and of Latin literature. With English and German humanists he was agreed that this should be combined with religious instruction. Unlike the early humanists, however, he sought to subdue the minds of his pupils, not to liberate them. The Jesuit school did not exist to perfect the individual ; its purpose was to

[1] Issued by Aquaviva (General of the Order), in 1599.

mould the thought of the individual so that he would accept without question the dogmas of the Catholic Church. As it is put in the ' Spiritual Exercises ' the aim is to ' make us truly feel with the orthodoxy of the Church '. 3. He conceived of his Order as a company of knights who lived to serve the Blessed Virgin. Hence he laid stress on the value of military virtues, on implicit obedience, on a high sense of knightly 'honour'. He reverenced the monastic orders, and just as he drew certain elements from the best side of the various orders of knighthood, so he profited by the experience of monastic establishments. 4. He knew the University of Paris and he turned to good account what he had learned there. He owed yet more to the University of Louvain, to Vives whom he met in Bruges, and the humanistic schools of the Low Countries. 5. Lastly he was not too proud to learn from his enemies. In the ' higher schools ' (universities) he left the study of medicine to the Lutherans, since he felt he could not hope to rival them in this department of knowledge ; but he knew what Sturm had done and there is little doubt that he profited from Sturm's example. In other words Ignatius took hints from every system of education with which he was acquainted, and made use of the best elements in each, so far as they could be adapted to his own requirements. ' The Order ', says Paulsen, ' had mastered contemporary learning in all its branches: Renaissance culture and Scholasticism.'[1]

Before dealing with the purely religious elements in Jesuit education it is well to notice the changes introduced into the school curriculum.

It is true that the three lower classes studied

[1] Op. cit., p. 82.

' grammar ' and that the higher classes studied
' humanity ' and rhetoric ; that thus the *matter* studied
in a Jesuit College was much the same as it was in
Sturm's Academy or in an English Grammar School.
But the way in which lessons were given was different.
1. The teacher was a highly educated man. He had
undergone a prolonged training in philosophy and
theology and was a specialist in casuistry or ' moral
theology '. 2. Each teacher taught the same boys
throughout the whole of their school career. In each
of the six years which they spent in school, the master
' moved up ' with his class. In this way—apart altogether from the Confessional—he acquired a much
more intimate knowledge of his pupils than was
possible for teachers to whom a different set of boys
came each year. 3. The lessons were made as easy and
pleasant as possible. Much of the teaching took the
form of lectures. There was no dictation, and the
master was taught to awaken and retain the interest of
his pupils. The lessons were short and few. Physical
exercise, games (indoor and outdoor) occupied a
prominent place in the curriculum. 4. The teacher
never punished a boy. Such corporal punishment as
was given was inflicted by a special officer, the
' Corrector '. The teacher was taught to win the
affections of his pupils and to stir up their ambition.
Great use was made of ' rivalry ', of ' distinctions '
awarded for merit.

The curriculum was limited. Its aim was not so much
the acquisition of a large body of knowledge, as
cultivation of certain powers, in particular memory and
readiness of speech. To be quick-witted, to be able to
debate, to present a case in an easy and plausible

manner, was regarded as an invaluable quality in an
educated man. More than any other ' religious ', the
Jesuit was a man of the world. He was trained to feel
at ease in any society and at all times to keep not only
his feelings but even his features under perfect control.

The boy who left a Jesuit College was *thoroughly*
trained. The range of his knowledge was not wide : so
far as it went it was accurate. Constant ' repetition '
and annual examinations secured this.

## RELIGIOUS TRAINING

When we turn to the specifically religious side of
Jesuit education we are struck by certain characteristic
features. On one occasion, when bidding farewell to
certain members of the Order who were going to take
up an appointment in some distant place, Ignatius said :
' If only we educate the *heart* we need not trouble too
much about mere knowledge.' This saying became as it
were the watchword of the Order.

The Jesuit attached enormous importance to the
cultivation of the heart. 1. Mass was said daily—
wherever possible in the School Chapel. 2. Great stress
was laid on ' Holy ' Days. The boy's heart was stirred
by stories of heroic martyrs, of miracles wrought by
saints, of supernatural visions vouchsafed to saints. In
a Jesuit church the reliquaries (which contained the
relics of the saints) were adorned in the most sumptuous
way with gold and precious stones. The church itself,
and all its services, was made as magnificent and
impressive as possible. All this was deliberately
calculated to appeal at once to the senses and the
imagination of boys at an age when they were most

impressionable. 3. Great importance was attached to prayer. Every lesson began with prayer or with the sign of the Cross. Boys were trained to pray, to make frequent use of the Rosary, to spend between a quarter and half an hour each day, morning and evening, in private prayer. 4. Every boy went to confession and communion once a week. Great stress was laid on self-examination. ' Piae Meditationes' gave the scholar opportunity to examine the 'state of his heart'. He was taught to know his own heart, and the hearts of others. Teachers were told to busy themselves each night in ' examining the conscience' of individual pupils. 5. Before Festivals and the longer holidays there were ' Piae Cohortationes' at which addresses were given to stir up feelings of devotion. The addresses were sometimes given by scholars who were thus enabled at once to inspire their fellows and to improve their own Latin. 6. Above all there were the ' Exercitia Spiritualia'. There is no need to dwell at length on the Spiritual Exercises of St. Ignatius. Few books of devotion have had a deeper influence. Just as a soldier learns by constant drill to become a useful unit in an army, so the Christian soldier was trained by spiritual drill (exercises) to fight his spiritual battles.

To go through the Exercises properly requires a month. The first week is devoted to an inquiry into the state of the soul and ends with confession. The second presents a vivid picture of the two combatants, Christ and Satan, who fight for the soul of man ; and leads up to deliberate surrender of the will to Christ. The third recalls in the most vivid manner the incidents connected with the passion and death of Christ. The penitent is thus enabled to realize the meaning of sin and to recognize his share in the guilt which brought Christ to Calvary. The fourth deals with Christ's victory and glory. The penitent is filled with joy and gratefully vows that henceforth he will give himself utterly to God and prove his sincerity by amending his life.

Each meditation begins with preparatory prayer in which divine aid is sought to bring home to the imagination the figures and events on which meditation is based ; to impress on the heart the feelings such meditation is intended to arouse. Every side of man's nature is dealt with. The memory is stirred up to recall past sins. Emotion is aroused so that due contrition may be felt. The will is affected so that the penitent resolves to live aright and gladly to renounce every allurement of the world, the flesh and the devil. As we have said, the Jesuit practice is, wherever possible, to devote four weeks to the Exercises under the guidance of a skilled director. In the case of schoolboys the four weeks are reduced to one.

From what has been said it is obvious that no other body of men has put forth more strenuous efforts to mould the hearts and wills of their pupils than the Jesuits. This book is not an essay in controversial divinity : it is not the author's purpose to pass sentence on any particular system of theology. To some, the Jesuit attempt to gain complete control over a human being, so that he becomes a mere instrument in the hands of his superior, is little less than infamous. It involves the destruction of personality in any true sense of the term. To others it seems to be a magnificent effort conducted with unequalled patience and unrivalled skill to save an immortal soul.

The *Spiritual Exercises* became the principal means by which the Jesuits attained this goal of complete self-annihilation and absolute discipline, even in thought and feeling, and at the same time of absolute self-surrender to the glory of God and of the Church. The education of the other youths entrusted to the Colleges had of course the same object in view.[1]

Hitherto we have dealt with the ' education of the heart ' ; now let us turn to the training of the mind. The main instrument for doing this was the Catechism. The Society of Jesus is rich in catechetical literature, but perhaps their most important catechism is that produced by St. Peter Canisius.[2] We give a short account of this truly remarkable book, for no other catechism compares with it in the thoroughness with which it seeks to do its work. Protestants have used (some continue to use) catechisms ; but no Protestant has yet possessed a catechism which bears favourable comparison in depth and breadth with that of Canisius.

Canisius begins with the question : ' What is a Christian ? ' ' A Christian is one ', he makes answer, ' who holds fast to that which is wise and right.' Wisdom is defined as Faith, Hope and Love ; Righteousness or Justice, is to avoid evil and to do that which is good. This summary is expounded in six sections. The first section deals with Faith, which is defined as ' a gift of God and a light by which man being enlightened holds as true, and clings to, what is revealed of God through the Church '.

[1] Op. cit., p. 85.
[2] *Summa doctrinae et institutiones christianae* (1554). *Institutiones christianae pietatis* (1566). See also James Brodrick : *St. Peter (Canisius)*, 1935. O. Braumsberger : *Enstehung und erste Entwicklung der Catechismen des seligen Petrus Canisius* (1893).

The Christian Faith is summed up in the Apostles' Creed. The use of the Creed is explained and the first four articles (down to ' suffered under Pontius Pilate ') expounded. At this point Canisius turns aside to explain, at considerable length, why Christians make the sign of the Cross.

Questions 13-21 deal with the remaining articles, and the section ends with the question ' Is it enough for a Christian merely to believe what the Apostles' Creed contains ? ' No, is the answer, for in addition to the Creed there is the Bible, the Church, and what the Holy Spirit reveals through the Church.

The second section deals with Hope and the Lord's Prayer. Hope is defined as a ' virtue infused by God in virtue of which we await with sure confidence the blessings of Salvation and Eternal Life from God '. Hope is obtained through (a) prayer, (b) the daily consideration of God's benefits, (c) purity of conscience.

Then follows an exposition of the Lord's Prayer ; to one or other of whose seven petitions ' all forms and modes of prayer can be reduced '. All this is dealt with in fourteen questions. The remaining five questions are devoted to an exposition of the Angelic Salutation (Ave Maria). The Jesuits were famous for their devotion to the Blessed Virgin. It is not surprising, therefore, that exactly one half the space devoted to treatment of the Lord's Prayer is given to the Ave Maria. Here it may be convenient to point out one striking difference between Canisius and the authors of Protestant catechisms. The Protestant tries to support his statements by proofs from Scripture ; on the margin of the catechism references are given to texts in very much the same way as is done in the margin of the Authorized Version of the Bible. In this respect Canisius follows the Protestant example ; but in addition he quotes freely from the Fathers. In regard to the Virgin Mary the ' Testimony of the Fathers ' includes passages from Ambrose, Augustine, Bernard and Chrysostom.

The third section deals with Love and the Ten Commandments. Love is defined as ' a virtue infused by God, by means of which we love God and our neighbour aright '. Sixteen questions are devoted to the Commandments, and on the whole, the exposition is very much the same as that which we find in, let us say, Nowell's Catechism. There are, however, two striking differences. The eighth question runs as follows : ' Why do we revere and invoke the Saints ? ' The answer to this question is very long and very thorough. About two dozen passages are quoted from the Fathers to prove that the Saints love us, know all that we do, are intensely interested in our salvation. The $\lambda\alpha\tau\rho\epsilon\iota\alpha$ which is offered to the Saints is distinguished from the ' Worship ' that is offered to God. The Saints, and especially our patron Saints, intercede for us. Martyrs are to be commemorated. It is absurd to say, as is done ' by those who slander us ', that we deify the Saints.

The Jesuit was taught never to refer to a dead ' heresy ', or an ' idle ' speculation of some scholastic. He was taught never to be offensive in his references to those who differed from him. In Germany, for instance, he was told never to refer to a Lutheran as a ' heretic '. But he *was* taught to emphasize the truth (as he regarded it) as against the errors (without discussing them) of those who opposed the tenets of the Roman Church.

In the same way the ninth question deals, though more briefly, with another subject that was much discussed, the use of images and pictures. The orthodox Catholic, it is said, unlike the heathen, does not bow down to wood and stone ; he reverences Christ and the Saints who are represented to him in the pictures and images which adorn the church.

Having dealt with the Ten Commandments, Canisius proceeds to deal with another set of commandments, concerning which fierce controversy raged, viz. the five commandments of the Church. Certain festivals are to be kept, certain fasts are to be observed, auricular confession is to be made at least once a year, the Holy Communion is to be received (at least at Easter), Mass has to be attended (on days of obligation).

The Protestant maintained that Holy Scripture was in itself a sufficient guide for faith and conduct. The Catholic replied that Scripture *must* be supplemented by the teaching of the Church. The nineteen questions of this sub-section deal with this matter. Careful exposition is given of the Romanist view of the Church, and its traditions, and of Scripture. Here, as one might expect, many quotations from the Fathers and Doctors of the Church appear.

In the fourth section, which consists of fifteen questions, Canisius deals with the Sacraments. Each of the seven Sacraments is carefully explained ; but, as we might expect, attention is chiefly directed to the Eucharist. The doctrine of Transubstantiation, the nature of the sacrifice of the Mass, the reason for elaborate ceremonies, especially at great festivals, the

qualifications and powers of the priest—all these are
expounded with great care, at considerable length,
with constant reference to the Fathers.

The fifth section deals with the Christian conception
of Righteousness. It falls into two portions : we must
(a) avoid sin, and (b) do good.

Sin is of three kinds—original, mortal, venial. Why
sin must be avoided, and how sin may be avoided ;
the seven deadly sins ; the nine sins which we commit
when we share in the sins of others ; and the sins like
those of Sodom that cry aloud to Heaven : all this is
carefully discussed. This portion ends with consideration of the question how we may be cleansed from sin.

Canisius next turns his attention to good works
(Fasting, Prayer, Alms) ; the four cardinal virtues
(Wisdom, Justice, Temperance, Courage) ; the seven
fruits of the Spirit ; the Beatitudes. The section con-
cludes with reference to the ' Last Things ', Death,
Judgement, Heaven, Hell.

The sixth section deals with the establishment and
confirmation of the true Catholic Faith ; and treats
of the Nicene and Athanasian Creeds. It has many
references to the Fathers. In the smaller version of the
Catechism—the one with which we are concerned—
this section is omitted.

During the sixteenth century the hours at which the
catechism was taught varied from place to place. At
Cologne it was taught at four on Sunday afternoon.
At Rome on Fridays the juniors devoted half an hour
to the smaller catechism, the seniors to the larger.
In addition to all this, boys in the lower classes had a
lesson in the catechism every day, boys in the middle

school two or three times a week, boys in the top form once a week.

Such, then, was the religious education given in a Jesuit College in the early days of the Society. It is obvious that the aim of the Society was to furnish each boy with a body of knowledge which would enable him to give an account of the faith that was in him. He had a ready made system of ethics and theology in which everything was admirably clear and definite.

He knew—at least he was taught to believe that he knew—how to think and how to act. The way of life was clearly marked out for him. For six years his thoughts and feelings were carefully controlled by psychological experts who knew the inmost secrets of his heart, and who were determined to send the boy out into the world thoroughly convinced of certain truths, firmly resolved to lead a certain kind of life. ' Since the Revival of Learning ', says Quick, ' no body of men has played so important a part in education as the Jesuits.' The most hostile critic must admit that no body of men has striven harder to give religious education, as the Roman Catholic understands it, than the Jesuits.

# CHAPTER V

## *Comenius (Jan Amos Komenský) 1592-1671*

BACON, who is to be numbered amongst the greatest, if not amongst the noblest of Englishmen, left an indelible mark on science and philosophy ; he exerted an almost equal influence upon education. The men who introduced ' realism ' into education, and did so much to reform the school, were all inspired by him. Of these reformers Comenius is the greatest. He found the school ' the terror of boys, the slaughter-house of the mind ', he showed men how to make it a very different place.

In the first flush of German Humanism, Melancthon exclaimed, ' Of what importance it is to Christ's Church that boys be rightly instructed in grammar ! ' In the hands of his degenerate successors Latin Grammar became not only the dreariest drudgery ; it was the knife which the butcher used to do his work in what Comenius so well described as the ' slaughter-house of the mind '. Speaking of schoolmasters in the year 1610 a gentleman of the name of Schupp said, ' If I had a dog that I loved I would not hand him over to these beasts, much less a son.'

There were three articles in the creed of the new reformers.

(1) Knowledge of things is primary ; knowledge of words is secondary. Schools in which only languages are taught miss their true object. ' Be not wrapt up in

the past ', said Bacon, ' there is an actual present lying all about you, look up, and behold it in its grandeur.'

(2) The present is greater than the past. It is a mistake to assume that all true philosophy and all true science is to be met with in classical antiquity and there alone. ' As far as real knowledge is concerned ', said Bacon, ' we are the classics ourselves, having surpassed the ancients by wider experience and profounder thinking.'

(3) Granted that linguistic study is desirable, the method of such study must be radically reformed. ' Any camp follower, tramping with an army into foreign lands, picked up enough in the course of a few months to express himself fluently in several foreign languages, whilst boys who were taught Latin by learning grammar and not by practical use spent ten years in studying a language which they failed to master.'

Comenius, by far the most distinguished of such reformers, made no claim to be original : he owed a good deal to Ratke. ' For though ', says Keatinge, ' in point of attainment he was undoubtedly one of the most remarkable men of his time, he was amongst the most humble.' 'Christ my Lord knows ', he says in the preface to one of his books, ' that my heart is so simple that it matters not to me whether I teach or be taught, act the part of teacher of teachers, or disciple of disciples. What the Lord has given me I send forth for the common good.'

In his eyes the final aim of all education is religious. ' As the restoration of man to the Paradise which he forfeited, and to the image of God which he lost, is the aim of the providence of God in Christ, so the aim of the school is that restoration, a bringing of its work and methods into a harmony with moral and religious aims, and subordinating the school to the Church as a Spiritual Society."[1]

In a short study of one aspect of Comenius' educational work it is impossible to trace his chequered career ; to follow him from his native Bohemia, whence he was expelled through Jesuit influence ; to Poland, where he did so much of his educational work ; to England, where but for the Civil War he would have established his *Collegium pansophicum*, a clearing-house of ideas to which all learned men in Europe were to contribute ; to Sweden, where he was asked by the Government to reform the schools ; to Holland, where he died. It is impossible to deal with his theological writings ; his pastoral activities—he was a Bishop of the Moravian Church—his work for peace between church and church and between state and state. Nor is it possible, as one would like to do, to show the influence exerted on him by one of the most pathetic figures in the history of education—Ratke, or Ratichius, brilliant, devout, quarrelsome, of whom Laurie says, ' There are few of the now recognized rules of method which will not in substance be found in his writings.' For all such information the reader must turn to the splendid work that has been done on Comenius by Keatinge and by Laurie, or to the famous history of education by von Raumer. Indeed after reminding the reader that the earliest books of Comenius deal with the reformed method of teaching Latin and mentioning his three most celebrated books, we must turn to our subject proper.

[1] S. S. Laurie : *J. A. Comenius*, p. 92.

(1) The most popular of all his works is *Orbis Pictus*. Things, he insisted, must come before words ; where one cannot show a thing one must show its picture. ' For it is certain ', he says in the preface, ' that there is nothing in the understanding, which has not previously been in the sense ; consequently to exercise the senses carefully in discriminating the differences of natural objects is to lay the foundation of all wisdom, all eloquence, and all good and prudent action.'

(2) His most famous work, *Janua Linguarum Reserata sive Seminarium Linguarum et Scientiarum omnium* (The Gate of Tongues unlocked or a Seminary of the Tongues and all Sciences), was translated into almost every European language as well as into Arabic and Russian. ' For many generations ', it is said, ' the school boys of three continents thumbed this book.'

(3) His greatest book is *Didactica Magna*, first written in Czech (1632), which remained unpublished until 1849, when it was recovered from the archives of Lissa.

## Comenius on Religious Education

It is not a little disappointing that one who contributed so much to Method in other departments has given us so little help in our efforts to discover the best method of imparting religious truth. ' Comenius gives great prominence to this part of his Didactic (i.e. to his Method as applied to Piety)' , says Laurie, ' and treats it at considerable length ; but it cannot be said that Method in any strict application of that term is successfully exhibited in its relation to religious instruction. The chapter on this subject is in reality a series of propositions in which the order of Christian doctrinal teaching is laid down, and to some extent the manner of it.' That Laurie's estimate is as just as it is shrewd will appear from the Syllabus which Comenius drew up for use in a " Pansophic School ".

For the whole school there are to be hymns, Bible readings and prayers. In the first class (we omit the Latin names given to the different forms) ' religious exercises ' consist of (a) the ' heads of the catechism ', (b) a few short hymns and prayers.

In Class 2 the catechism is to be thoroughly learned.

Class 3 is to specialize on the ' famous deeds ' recorded in the Biblical narrative.

Class 4 is to make use of a special collection of hymns and psalms. It is to have an ' epitome of the New Testament ', i.e. a continuous account of the life of Christ and His Apostles drawn from the four Gospels. In this class the Greek Testament is introduced.

Class 5. In addition to hymns, psalms and prayers, this class is to use a text-book. *The Gate of the Sanctuary,* as it was called, was an abbreviated version of Scripture history. It was so arranged that the whole book could be read in one year. Throughout the book the text of Scripture and that alone was used.

In Class 6 the whole Bible was read.

In Class 7 the ' most devotional psalms and hymns of the Church ' were studied. Prayers were to be of a special character, and were to be drawn from (a) Scripture, (b) inspired theologians, (c) sainted martyrs. A ' compendium of Christian beliefs, duties, hopes, expressed in Biblical phraseology ' was to be read daily. In this class the text-book was to deal with ' the last stage of wisdom on earth, i.e. communion of souls with God '. This includes (a) The ' Ascent of the mind to God ' ; the whole universe was surveyed, and the boy was shown how ' heaven and earth and all therein tell the glory of God '. (*b*) The ' Formal Part ' or the ' Key to the Bible ' ; that is to say a series of practical rules for reading the Scriptures with profit and for duly considering the works of God. The Bohemian Brethren, as we have already seen, were the first to produce a catechism, and it is almost certain that this simple Czech Catechism was the one which Comenius used. It is important, however, to note that though Comenius believed in dogmatic instruction, based on the catechism, he differed from most Lutherans, Calvinists and Anglicans of his time in that he did not teach the catechism in a purely mechanical way. As we have seen he began with the ' heads of the catechism ', that is, presumably with the simpler questions, and only after these had been studied for a year did he proceed to those which were more complex. Indeed, we may claim that Comenius was the father of the ' graded method ' ! His hymns were ' graded ' as were his prayers and his Bible readings. He was the first to use a ' shortened ' Bible.

For reasons into which we need not enter, the Lutheran sang hymns for two hundred years before they were introduced into the Church of England. The Lutheran child has been ' brought up ' on hymns in a way that until the nineteenth century was unknown in England or Scotland. Yet it was not a Lutheran, it was a Czech, who was the first to realize the great part which hymns, when carefully selected and explained, may play in religious education. In this respect, Comenius was at least three hundred years ahead of his English contemporaries. Only in very recent times, indeed, has the hymn come into its own in the English

School. Comenius, we may say, was the first great educationist to study and understand the principles of ' School Worship '.

He was not, indeed, the first to realize the effect on the child of the Bible story. Others anticipated him in that respect ; but he was convinced that every child should know the ' famous deeds ' recorded in Scripture. In other words, he realized that a child gains more through being introduced to a noble and inspiring personality than by being taught dogmatic theology. ' As in every class ', he says, 'History, as the eye of life, should find a place, so that all that is most memorable in the past both in deed and word may be known,' so Bible stories not only awaken interest, they teach lessons that otherwise might not be learned.

Finally Comenius believed that Bible reading has a technique of its own.    In his *Key to the Bible* he showed how the Bible might be read with profit.    The Protestant was ready enough to denounce the Romanist for believing that the Sacrament acts on man in a magical manner by virtue of its own inherent force (*ex opere operato*) ;  he did not always remember that in this respect Holy Scripture and Sacrament are alike. Comenius saw this clearly. There is a right way and there is a wrong way of reading the Bible, and it is of the first importance that we should learn to read the Bible aright.    If we do this we shall experience the ' Ascent of the mind to God ' :  we shall realize that ' heaven and earth and all therein tell the glory of God '.

Like every other who has studied the question, Comenius felt the paradox that lies at the very heart of religious education. Religion *must* be taught and yet it *cannot* be taught. It is the gift of God.

' Piety ', he says, ' is the gift of God through the Holy Ghost ' ; ' yet ', he continues, ' as the Spirit commonly acts through ordinary means such as parents, teachers, pastors, it is right to consider the method of the duties of those instruments.' Surely he is right : any other view must end in fatalism.

Like Luther, Comenius believed that there are three means by which one develops not only into a theologian but even into an ordinary Christian ;

(1) Meditation—on the words, works and goodness of God.

(2) Prayer (perpetua ad Deum suspiratio).

(3) Self-examination (2 Cor. xiii. 5).

We have examined the syllabus which Comenius drew up for use in a ' Pansophic ' School ; we must now glance at the seven rules which he drew up for the guidance of parents and teachers.

(1) The good seed must be sown in infancy.

(2) From the very first the child must be taught to express devotion by means of bodily actions. He must ' bend his knees ', ' look up to heaven ', and so forth.

(3) All lessons in school must be directed to an *eternal* goal.

(4) Those who reach Heaven are those who in their earthly life (*a*) had God continually before their eyes, (*b*) feared Him, and (*c*) kept His commandments.

(5) Children must be taught to refer (directly or indirectly) to God all that they hear, do, or suffer.

(6) From their earliest years they must be taught to concern themselves with the things that lead to God— Scripture, Prayer, Good Works.

(7) In every Scripture lesson the child must be taught (1) to believe what God has revealed, (2) to do

what God has commanded, (3) to hope for what God has promised.

Boys are to be guarded against evil examples and are to be ' exhorted to keep the way of the Cross as the most secure way ' : but since ' because of the imperfection of their nature they can do no good thing ', they must be taught to ' rely on the perfection of Christ, the Lamb of God that taketh away the sin of the world '. ' On Him we must call and Him we must trust. We shall thus have finally placed the hope of our salvation in safety, when we have laid the burden on Christ, the corner stone.'

## MORAL TRAINING

The 24th chapter of the Didactic deals with the ' Method of instilling Piety ' ; the 23rd, which contains eighteen rules, is devoted to the ' Method of Morals '. Like Aristotle, Comenius believed that virtue is learned by continually doing what is right (Rule 8). He complains that the teachers of his day—who can claim that their successors have altogether escaped their weakness ?—set about their task in the wrong way. ' No one ', he says, ' seeks to form the morals by working on the inward sources of action, but by purely external explanations and analysis of the virtues a superficial veneer of morality is given.'

' That only I call a school ', he says, ' where minds are instructed in wisdom to penetrate all things, where souls and their affections are guided to the universal harmony of the virtues, and hearts are allured to divine love—*ubi omnes omnia omnino doceantur.*'

All virtues, he says, must be implanted in youth ;

but first of all the four cardinal virtues, Prudence, Temperance, Fortitude and Justice.

(1) Sound judgement is the foundation of all virtue.

(2) Throughout their school life the young must be taught temperance in eating and drinking, in sleep and waking, in labour and play, in speaking and keeping silent. Here, as elsewhere, the Golden Rule is *Ne quid nimis.*

(3) Boys must learn fortitude by overcoming themselves, i.e. by checking their desire to run about and play beyond the proper time ; by restraining their impatience, their grumbling, their anger. ' Under fortitude we include an honourable frankness of speech and a tolerance of labour.'

(4) Justice is learnt by doing harm to no one, by giving to each his own, by avoiding lying and deceit, by being generally serviceable and amiable. Under Justice is included promptitude and alacrity in serving others. Boys must learn that they are born not for themselves alone, but for God and their fellow men.

Such, in brief outline, is education as Comenius conceived it. To him the world was ' a seed plot, a boarding house, a training school, for man '. His destination is eternity. To prepare himself for eternity he must ascend three steps : *Se et secum omnia, nosse ; regere ; et ad Deum dirigere.* In other words he must (*a*) know all things, (*b*) have power over all things, including himself, (*c*) refer himself and all things to God, the source of all. All this may be summed up in three words, (*a*) Knowledge (Eruditio), (*b*) Virtue (Virtus seu Mores Honesti), (*c*) Piety (Religio seu Pietas). God is the *summum bonum*, the end of all man's striving.

It is difficult to exaggerate the services which Comenius rendered to the cause of education. Alike in German Gymnasium and in English Grammar School the classical and religious training, product at once of the Renaissance and the Reformation, had degenerated into something very like mere pedantry. Comenius brought, as it were, a fresh breath of life into classrooms in which the air had been breathed so long by so many that it had lost almost all its oxygen. Like the Jesuits, he realized that religious education worthy of the name means more than instruction ; it is the development of personality. Under the influence of Bacon he felt that there were no heights of knowledge to which man might not hope to reach. Inspired by faith he was persuaded that even the humblest might hope some day to become in character like God. In a word it is the grandeur of his conceptions which places Comenius amongst the very greatest of those who have written on education in general and on religious education in particular.

# CHAPTER VI

## *Pietism*

WE have reached a stage at which we may fitly pause at once to look back on the road along which we have travelled, and to catch a glimpse of the direction which the rest of our inquiry is likely to take. Modern education begins with Humanism ; modern religious education begins with Christian Humanism. In other words, in education, religion and the highest known culture must be combined. But Christian Humanism in its earliest form was unable to solve our problem ; and that for three reasons.

(1) The synthesis which Erasmus made of classical antiquity and the Christian religion was of such a kind that it did justice neither to the one element nor to the other. His view of Christianity was superficial, his picture of the ancient world unreal.

(2) It was easy enough to find men who could teach the Latin language ; it was exceedingly difficult to discover men who were at once able to assimilate the thought of the ancient writers and to convey their spirit. Sturm was a great exception : in the hands of the average teacher ' learning Latin ' was reduced to a mechanical, sometimes even to a soul-destroying, process.

(3) The appearance of two new phenomena, the Reformation and the beginnings of modern science completely changed the situation. For almost two

centuries religion was the main interest of men's lives ;
the violent disputes to which different interpretations
of religion led forced men to study the Bible afresh.
For if God had spoken to man, and if the record of His
self-revelation is presented in the Bible, then from the
Bible as from nothing else man must learn to live aright.
The Bible must, therefore, be made intelligible to all ;
its teaching must be reduced to some sort of system.
Hence theology, chiefly in the form of catechetical
instruction, occupies a large place in the school
curriculum. For two hundred years the intellectual
side of Christianity is presented at the expense of the
emotional. Boys are introduced to the deepest theological problems at an age at which it is impossible
for them to understand them. They are taught results ;
they are not shown how these results are reached. In a
word, theology is cultivated at the expense of religion.
Hence the value of the Jesuit contribution. The Jesuit
insists that through religious education the whole
personality (not merely the mind) shall be developed,
and that this development shall take place in congenial
surroundings.

Comenius introduces ' Realism ' into the school.
Henceforward men will have to make a new synthesis :
science and religion will have to come to terms. This
problem will receive much attention in the nineteenth
century ; a solution of the problem has not yet been
reached. Like the Jesuits, Comenius feels that education
deals with the whole of man's personality. Yet in
Comenius and the Jesuits alike something is lacking.
Comenius once described the school as a factory in
which men are made. The Jesuit tried to make men ;
but he made them in his own image rather than in the

image of God. Each human being, we now believe, is a separate entity which contains within itself the laws of its own development. No teacher can make men ; he can only help them to develop their personalities. This great principle we shall find expressed in the work of Pestalozzi. His way was prepared for him by the views which led up to, and were expressed in, the French Revolution. He owed much to Rousseau, one of the most remarkable figures in the history of education ; he owes much also to less known men, with two of whom we shall deal presently. To Pestalozzi we owe the best method, so far as we have yet learnt it, of giving religious education. But though his method is splendid, his view of religion is imperfect. He can tell us *how* to teach, he cannot tell us *what* to teach. For answer to that problem we must turn to another, to the man who above all others faced the question, ' What *is* this religion that we attempt to teach ? '

Having thus learned what we can in regard to the method and the content of religious education from the greatest men who have dealt with these subjects, we shall return to our own country and seek to show how this has been done in England.

The problem to which Pietism addressed itself was this. Granted that mere knowledge of theology is not only inadequate but almost worthless as a means of developing Christian character, how can religion, which is a matter of the heart, be brought to bear on boys and girls in school ? For answer to this question we must turn to two men, Francke and Zinzendorf. But in order to understand their answer we must bear in mind the conditions under which they did their work.

(1) The Thirty Years' War and the effect it had on Germany. For this we must ask our readers to turn to Ward (*Cambridge Modern History*, Vol. IV, pp. 417 ff.) who gives a vivid description of the material damage done. Agriculture and trade were ruined ; two-thirds of the entire population perished or emigrated. The moral effect on all classes was that of a ' deadly blight '. Nobles and well-to-do burghers gave way to ' a reckless-ness in the conduct of life, manifesting itself in many ways, but most alarmingly in a wholly unrestrained self-indulgence '. ' In the midst of this social chaos, religion, in whose name these iniquities were perpe-trated, was trampled in the mire.' The Village Schools were for the most part swept away ' by the storms of the war '. In the ' Latin ' (or Grammar) Schools, ' a new influence was needed to animate a system of teaching hardened and narrowed by confessional jealousy, and by the long-continued subordination of all intellectual effort to theological ends.'

Of the universities Paulsen says :

> University life, at this time, presents a lamentable aspect. . . . The students had sunk to the deepest depths, and carousals and brawls, carried to the limits of brutality and bestiality, largely filled their days. Even the professors, by reason of their dependence and poverty, seem frequently to have been pulled down into the mire.

Francke was born fifteen years after the War ended ; throughout the greater part of his lifetime many of its degrading effects survived.

(2) The Rise of Pietism. Pietism has an interesting

history. It derives in part from English Puritans and from Dutch ' Precisionists ' ; in its later form, however (in which through Methodism and the Evangelical revival it returns to England), its father is Philipp Spener (1635-1705). Spener was a Lutheran clergyman who was deeply distressed at the appalling state into which religion had fallen in his country. He strove to amend it in two ways.

First, he persuaded some of the more serious members of his congregation to meet together (at first in his own house : later in larger assemblies) to discuss religious questions in a devotional spirit. This meeting which combined prayer, praise and testimony, with Bible reading and exposition, was called the *collegium pietatis*. Following Spener's example a few like-minded clergymen introduced *collegia pietatis* into their parishes. The movement spread, though the great majority of the clergy were strongly opposed to it.

Secondly, he wrote a book in which he bewailed the lamentable state of religion and morals in the Lutheran Church and suggested six ways in which improvement might be effected.[1]

Pietist (goody-goody) was the nickname given to Spener's followers who were regarded with as much hostility by the average Lutheran pastor as Methodist ' enthusiasm ' was by the typical Anglican parson in the eighteenth century.[2] Bismarck, who knew more of political expediency, than of Christian principle, once described a Pietist as a man who played the hypocrite in religion to make a career.

[1] *Pia Desideria.*
[2] A splendid bibliography will be found in H. Leube : *Church Hist.*, Vol. 4.

## AUGUST HERMANN FRANCKE (1663-1727)

Francke,[1] who was a precocious child, grew up in a devout home in comfortable conditions. He had a brilliant academic career, and won fame at Leipzig, as a university lecturer. His conversion, of which he himself has given a full description, is often referred to. Having to preach on the text, ' But these are written that ye might believe that Jesus is the Christ : and that believing ye might have life through his name,' he discovered that he was far from certain how much of the truth he was about to proclaim he actually believed. After passing through an intense struggle he emerged a happy believer. Abandoning every desire for scholarly distinction he threw himself with almost indescribable energy into the service of his Master. He became a Pietist of the Pietists. For this he suffered severely. Condemned by the orthodox clergy, he had to leave more than one parish. At last, however, he was appointed Professor of Theology in the newly founded University of Halle ; he had a crown living in the city, and established an orphanage which for generations was the most famous in the world. At his death upwards of 2,000 children were being educated in his schools, and from the University at least 5,000 clergymen had gone out into the world, if not exactly to disseminate his views, at least profoundly influenced by the training they had received at his hands.

When Francke arrived in Halle he found the children in his parish wild and ignorant. Parents cared nothing for education ; their great ambition was to see their children earn a few coppers at the earliest possible age.

[1] G. Kramer : *A. H. Francke Ein Lebensbild*, 1880-2.

Nor had parents much control over their lawless brood.

It was the custom of the time for the poor of the parish to present themselves each Thursday morning at the Pastor's house to receive alms. When they came, Francke invited them into his house, and for a quarter of an hour examined the children who came with them on their religious knowledge in general and their knowledge of Luther's catechism in particular. Horrified at their ignorance, he determined to start a school in his own house. Certain citizens heard of this and asked that their children might be allowed to attend it. A little later one or two noblemen asked if their children might become boarders in Francke's house. From these small beginnings the great educational institutions arose. Within six years after Francke's arrival 600 children were being educated in his schools, and 101 orphans were being taken care of in his orphanage. Three years previously a great building was erected to which he transferred the whole of his institutions. It still stands on the splendid site he chose for it. His foresight was rewarded ; the orphanage was well supplied with water and had abundance of fresh air. Cholera ravaged Halle more than once : but the ' Angel of Death ' passed the orphanage by.

Francke himself had no money ; the large sums he needed for the maintenance of his institutions came, he said, in answer to prayer (though his opponents said that he was a past-master in the art of propaganda). Gifts of money and land were managed with extraordinary care. Sales of stock and farm produce ; sales of a celebrated medicine which was made in the orphanage *Apotheke*, and used all over the world (this brought in several thousand pounds a year) ; printing and publishing ; these produced the large revenue required to build and maintain the orphanage and the ever-increasing schools.

With Francke's heavy work as parish priest and university professor we cannot deal. Nor can we tell how he anticipated such institutions as the British and Foreign Bible Society in translating the Scriptures into foreign tongues ; nor yet again how he trained missionaries and supported them (The ' Danish-Halle ' mission was the pioneer Protestant Foreign Mission). Few men have worked harder than Francke. The reason for his ceaseless activity on behalf of so many causes he stated on his death-bed : ' My faithful Jesus I have given myself to Thee soul and body ; that is sure.'

We are concerned solely with Francke as an educationist ; and before we consider in detail his various schools we must call attention to the fact that in one respect his position is absolutely unique. In the schools which he founded he was hampered by no tradition ; he had no Governing Body to control him. Neither Church nor State interfered with him (he stood in high favour with the King). He was absolutely independent of *all* external authority. He could teach his 2,000 children as he pleased and what he pleased. Thus he was able as no other teacher—at least none known to the present writer—has ever been able to do, to carry his own views into practice. His schools were founded by *himself*; they were founded simply and solely for religious ends. They existed for *one* purpose ; the whole curriculum was directed to *one* end—to make boys and girls religious.

## THE PAEDAGOGIUM

The Paedagogium was a boarding school for the sons of the nobility and gentry (as a rule the boys numbered about seventy), and was controlled by a superintendent and eight masters. The premises were large and airy, the supervision strict. In many ways it resembled the typical Grammar School of the period to be met with in England or Germany ; it differed, however, in the following respects. (1) Every boy learnt French and many boys learnt English or Italian. There was a French ' Hofmeister ' who supervised the manners of the boys and taught them to behave like gentlemen. French was spoken at meals. Boys had to learn to speak as well as to read a foreign language. (2) Much more attention was given to history and geography than in other schools. Francke believed firmly in the use of maps and models. (3) As many of the boys were destined to own or manage estates they were taught mensuration and those branches of Economics that are specially concerned with the management of land. (4) To Francke games seemed a waste of time. As a substitute for games boys received manual training in woodwork, metal work and the making of glass. Botany they learnt on the constant excursions they made through the surrounding countryside. They were taken to factories that they might see with their own eyes how things were made. There was a Natural History Museum in the school. (It may still be seen in the Orphanage.) Boys did some biology. They even learnt a little anatomy from dissecting dogs. They were taught the Greek Testament, and like all other boys of the period were trained to acquire an accurate and graceful Latin style. In the eighteenth century that was still regarded as essential. But as distinguished from the average Grammar School, which specialized in Latin, the boys who lived in the Paedagogium had to learn to read and to speak their mother-tongue correctly and to detect the qualities of good style as revealed in the literature of their own country. They had to read such newspapers as there were in those days, both in French and German ; they had to discuss their contents. Francke's aim was to fit his pupils to take an intelligent part in any discussion that might arise in cultivated society.

### THE GRAMMAR SCHOOL

Two-thirds of the boys who attended the Grammar School were drawn from the middle class (fees were lower than in the Paedagogium) ; the other third were drawn from the more promising pupils in the Orphanage. At first the school consisted of about 200 boys ; later on the numbers rose to about 400. (Here, as throughout Francke's institutions, there was a parallel school for girls for every one for boys.) Most of the boys who attended the Grammar School expected to go on to the University, many of them were intended for the Church ; the chief difference therefore between the Grammar School and the Paedagogium was that in the former Hebrew took the place assigned to French in the latter. Yet, like the Paedagogium, Francke's Grammar Schools differed from all other schools of the period in the following respects :

(a) The number of subjects studied at the same time was strictly limited. Francke insisted that it was better for a few things to be done thoroughly than that a larger number should be done in a superficial manner.

Knowledge, however limited, should be clear and definite, not vague and nebulous.

(*b*) There were no ' Class Lists ' arranged in order of merit. Co-operation was encouraged, rivalry of every kind forbidden.

(*c*) What the Germans call the *Fachsystem* was introduced for the first time. A boy in the fourth form, for instance, who was especially good at mathematics, would join the fifth form for lessons in that particular subject. The class system was made as elastic as possible to enable a boy to learn each subject as a member of that particular group with which he was best fitted to work.

(*d*) Considerable attention was devoted to music, both vocal and instrumental.

## THE ELEMENTARY SCHOOL

In contrast to the schools of the time, which for the most part were in a deplorable condition, Francke's Elementary Schools were admirable institutions. Every child had to learn to read with a cultivated accent— great stress was laid on this ; to do simple sums ; to write a good hand ; to acquire an elementary know- ledge of certain arts and crafts ; to sing. Constant repetition, frequent examinations, guaranteed that whatever was learnt was learnt thoroughly. Here as elsewhere Francke insisted that there was to be no half-knowledge. To him vague ideas were intolerable. Just as the Paedagogium was intended to fit the land- owner for his future responsibilities, the Grammar School the future professional man for the University ; so the Elementary School was definitely intended to prepare the humbler members of society for success in whatsoever branch of industry or service their future lot was to be cast.

In the Elementary School four periods out of every seven were devoted to scriptural (and religious) study. As little punishment as possible was used : Francke insisted throughout his life that the regulating principle in every school was to be love.

Perhaps this indicates as clearly as anything else the ideal that Francke always kept in view. The atmosphere in each of his schools was to be a religious atmosphere. Everything was to be done, and done consciously, to the Glory of God.

Pietism differed from contemporary Orthodoxy by insisting that in the sphere of religion mere knowledge was totally inadequate.[1] Religion involves more than correct belief, it demands ardent love and faithful service. In technical language Pietism laid far less emphasis than Orthodoxy on cognition ; it laid much greater emphasis on emotion and volition. In no schools which have ever existed was so much time devoted to Bible reading ; yet the Bible was never read without careful exposition and exhortation. Every passage was applied to life. Every child was taught to ask himself the question, ' In what respect does this particular passage apply to me ? ' At the University Francke replaced the old scholastic theology by ' Biblical Theology '. The Bible reading in his schools had always a practical end in view.

The same holds good in the case of the catechism. In every German school Luther's Catechism was supposed to be taught. Often, however, it was taught

[1] Was ist ein Pietist ?  Der Gottes Wort studiert
Und nach demselben auch ein heiliges Leben fuehrt.

in a superficial and indifferent way. So long as the
correct answers were given the average schoolmaster
was perfectly satisfied.   Francke completely revolution-
ized this system. Every class went through Luther's
Catechism once a week. He himself was a magnificent
catechist. As his schools increased in numbers he ceased
to teach ; but he never gave up his catechizing.
Twenty years daily practice with children of every age
served to perfect his method. Perhaps the easiest way
for us to understand his method is to turn to the
twenty-fifth chapter of George Herbert's *A Priest to the
Temple*. Herbert says that the skill of a catechist depends
on three things : the last of these he describes in the
following terms :

> When the answer sticks, in illustrating the thing by
> something else which he knows, making what he knows
> to serve him in that which he knows not : as when the
> parson once demanded, after other questions about
> man's misery, ' Since man is so miserable, what is to
> be done ? ' and the answerer could not tell, he asked
> him again what he would do if he were in a ditch.
> This familiar illustration made the answer so plain,
> that he was even ashamed of his ignorance ;  for he
> could not but say that he would haste out of it as fast
> as he could. Then he proceeded to ask whether he
> could get out of the ditch alone, or whether he needed
> a helper, and who was that helper. At sermons and
> prayers men may sleep or wander ; but when one
> is asked a question, he must discover what he is.

Francke asked all sorts of questions : in doing so he
tried to make the catechism *live*. He illustrated each
point not merely by reference to the child's daily life,
but by copious use of Scripture stories. In other words,

his method was inductive. He collected material from Holy Scripture and showed how it issued in the doctrine of the catechism : he took the catechism and showed in turn how it threw light on Holy Scripture.

Much the same method was used when dealing with praise and prayer. The child was taught that it is not enough to praise God with the lips, we must praise with the understanding also. The hymns sung in the school service were *explained* to children. Worship had to be intelligent, not purely mechanical.

So, too, with prayer. Each child was taught to pray, was taught to make use of extemporary prayer. Francke felt that any one who depended entirely on a Prayer Book would never learn to pray from the heart. Even the youngest has to discover for himself his own needs (chiefly from the study of Scripture), and to learn to frame petitions for the satisfaction of those needs in his own words.

In Francke's schools the time devoted to spiritual exercises was unusually great. According to his way of thinking the whole object of religious education was to train boys and girls to offer themselves body, soul and spirit as a ' living sacrifice ' to God.

## THE STAFF

Francke did not believe in large classes. At his death, for 2,200 children he had no fewer than 183 teachers and superintendents. How, it may be asked, did he obtain his staff, in an age when competent teachers were few and far between, and there was no training college for teachers ?

He lived in a University town in which poor students abounded. He said to a number of his own students,

' If you will teach in my school for two hours a day
I will give you dinner.' The breakfast of the middle
class German is a light one ; his supper a movable
feast which varies in quantity ; his dinner is the main
meal of the day. A free dinner was a great consideration
to a poor student. To others who taught for four hours
a day Francke gave not only a dinner but a little money.
He insisted, however, that no student should teach for
a long period on end. It is easy to grow tired ; a tired
teacher merely serves to weary his pupils. If it be asked
how Francke was able to form a competent staff out of
such unpromising material, the answer is that he was
peculiarly fortunate in acquiring the assistance of
certain able and devoted men who acted as ' superintendents '. Every teacher had to keep a ' log-book '
in which he recorded all that he did. Every week
there was a staff meeting. At this the log-books were
examined and methods were discussed. Continuous
effort was made both by teacher and by superintendent
to see how the standard of teaching could be improved.
But further : out of the mass of men who taught in his
schools Francke selected a limited number who became
students in a training college which he instituted—the
first of its kind, so far as we can discover, to be met with
in any country in Protestant Europe. Francke always
maintained that the best training for his future profession which any clergyman could receive was to be
acquired by teaching in some school. Most of his
teachers intended to become pastors ; but after the
Training College was thoroughly established a number
of men chose schoolmastering as their profession.
Within a few years these men were to be found doing
admirable work all over Germany. Francke had many

disappointments. Many of the students he tried were found to be utterly unfitted both by character and temperament for teaching children. Many, however, realized his two-fold ideal : a teacher of religion must be a devout believer in Jesus Christ ; he must be carefully trained to do his work in the best possible way.

## CONCLUSION

Such, then, was religious education as Francke conceived it ; such the system which obtained at Halle not only throughout his lifetime but for long years after his death. In certain respects it commands our admiration.

(1) It is obvious that if religion is to become a vital factor in school life the teaching of religion cannot be relegated to a purely subordinate place. It must be a regulating principle. The cultivation of religion in any school makes heavy inroads on the teacher's time and attention.

(2) Religious education must be given by trained teachers who are convinced believers in the religion they profess.

(3) The primal purpose of religious education is not so much to increase knowledge as to train and strengthen the affections and the will ; for the end of all religious education is to enable those who receive it to lead a godly life.

Yet there is another side to the picture. Economists tell us that the cultivation of land is subject to the ' law of diminishing returns '. Up to a certain point each additional ' dose ' of Capital and Labour results in increased production ; the time soon comes, however, when further ' doses ' of Capital and Labour do not yield correspondingly increased results. It may well be that this ' natural law ' obtains in the spiritual world ; that the human soul, like the soil, is subject to this law of all husbandry. Francke did not know, as we know to-day, the great part played by games in the mental and moral development of the child. Psychologists like Piaget have shown, since Francke's time, how much children learn from ' play '. Yet Francke had read the works of Horace, and it would have been well if he had remembered one verse in which that shrewd worldling tells of the need for recreation. ' Nor does Apollo always stretch his bow.'[1] It is impossible for any human being to live continuously in the rarefied atmosphere of the spiritual mountain top. Man is but man ; on earth at least he can never be pure spirit. His body must rest from labour ; his spiritual muscles must relax. ' Dulce est desipere in loco.' It is not only sweet : it is essential. After great spiritual effort must come rest ; the keenest boy cannot be always ' on his toes '.

To-day there is far too little Bible reading ; in Francke's schools there was too much. Spiritual digestion, like physical digestion, has its limits. Francke imposed spiritual burdens on young children which they were not able to bear. Some of them became prigs ; others revolted against religion of which in youth they had heard so much. Yet many grew up to be devoted Christians.

[1] *Hor. Carm.* II, 10, 19, 20.

# CHAPTER VII

## *Count Nicolaus Ludwig Zinzendorf (1700-1760) and the Moravian Schools*

UNTIL ten years ago Zinzendorf had not received the attention which as a reformer of religious education he deserved. For this there were two reasons. (1) In his lifetime his many eccentricities had prejudiced people against anything he said or did. In particular some of his two thousand hymns,[1] contained expressions which all regret and none can justify. (2) Until a certain scholar had ransacked the Moravian archives his views on education were unknown and inaccessible.

The son of a noble who occupied a prominent position at the Saxon court, he lost his father almost in infancy and was brought up under strong religious influence by his maternal grandmother, a noble specimen of the Pietist aristocrat. When he was ten he was sent to Halle and remained in Francke's Paedagogium for six years. Already he instinctively felt (in later years it became a firm conviction) that every child is born to be happy and that in education play is no less essential than work. At Halle he had to work eleven hours a day (5 to 12 and 2 to 6), and there were no games. In after years he described this as ' slavery '. An ardent believer in liberty he thought it better for children to learn less and enjoy freedom than to be

---

[1] A. Knapp : *Geistliche Gedichte des Grafen von Zinzendorf* (1845). Zinzendorf : *Kirchenliederdichtung Hans-Gunther Huober* (1934).

compelled to fill their heads with knowledge that was for the most part useless in after life.

His family wished him to follow in his father's footsteps and to serve the State. With this end in view he studied law, travelled, and obtained an appointment at court. But his heart was not in Law ; and at the earliest possible moment he bought an estate near Dresden and settled down, determined, with three other friends (one was the village Pastor, a friend to whom he had presented the living) as a ' Union of Four Brethren ' to imitate Francke, i.e. to found an orphanage, to write and publish devotional literature and to work for foreign missions. Something, however, happened which changed the whole course of his life.

At the time when Luther began his work of reformation the ' Bohemian Brethren ' numbered 200,000. But through the Counter-Reformation the ' Brethren ', in so far as they formed a visible church in Bohemia and Moravia, were almost utterly destroyed. For many years, however, they continued to exist in Hungary and Poland. Even in Moravia itself a ' hidden seed ' preserved something of the beliefs and practices of their fathers. Of this ' Hidden Seed ' two families escaped from Moravia in 1722, and, at Zinzendorf's invitation, settled down on his estate. During the seven years which followed some 300 refugees made their way from Bohemia and Moravia to Berthelsdorf. There they built a town called Herrnhut. The number of settlers was increased by the advent of other refugees from various quarters (some of them cherished strange beliefs). Out of these mixed materials the Unitas Fratrum (Unity of the Brethren), as the Moravian Church is more correctly called, was formed or rather, shall we say, re-formed. At first Zinzendorf found his refugees a difficult body to handle. He was a somewhat eccentric aristocrat ; for the most part they were somewhat eccentric artisans. Zinzendorf knew little of them : they knew little of him. At times, despite his unbounded kindness, some of the refugees described him as ' The Man of Sin '. But one evening it is said, something like a miracle took place at a Communion Service. A change came over the turbulent refugees, which in later days they could only explain by saying, ' We learnt to love '. Henceforward the Gemeine, as they called themselves, the Congregation, the Brother-hood, formed a happy band of Christians. Years afterwards a visitor described it as an earthly paradise.

As to how the Unitas Fratrum, the most missionary of all churches, was at first connected with the Lutheran Church, how it spread, and how it eventually became a separate church, we have not space to tell. Throughout Zinzendorf's life he was its devoted leader. Of his friction with the Saxon Government, his exile, his extensive travels in Europe and America, his joys and sorrows, his overflowing generosity, which at one time brought him to the verge of bankruptcy, of the favour he found with princes (Frederick William I of Prussia persuaded him to be made a bishop, though four years later he resigned his office), of his work in England and Holland and America, this is no place to speak, for we are solely concerned with Zinzendorf as a pioneer of religious education.

## THE CATECHISM

When he was twenty-two Zinzendorf published a catechism. It was called ' Pure Milk ', consisted of

seventy-eight questions and answers, and was intended
to help mothers in the training of young children.

Anyone who reads this catechism will at once
recognize its revolutionary character. Instead of asking
how the sum and substance of doctrine can be presented in such a way that children can easily learn it
by heart, Zinzendorf asks himself the question, ' How
best can I lead a child to love and serve God, as He
is presented in Christ ? ' He begins with the child's
body and shows that it is the frail perishable dwelling-
place of the soul. As over against the body which is
born to perish, the soul is made for heaven, the home of
God. God is omnipotent as He is omnipresent. In the
Bible he has given us a book which tells us how to live.
The Fall is treated in the most literal way, for Eden
was a real place to Zinzendorf. There man ate the
forbidden fruit, and sickness and distress came into the
world. But Jesus came as a physician to heal the sick.
He does so still, for He is not dead. We obey His
commandments because we love Him. Happiness lies
in friendship with Jesus, in loving the Heavenly Father
and in showing our love by seeking to do His will.

Here at the very outset Zinzendorf reveals certain
views which he held through life. He does not invite
the child to come up on a platform where grown up
people sit ; he does not ask him to learn to speak as
grown up people do. He steps down from the platform
and stands beside the child. He looks at the world
through the child's eyes. To him, from first to last, the
child-like is the divine. Zinzendorf does not ask children
to speak like adults, to think like adults, to feel like
adults. There is a time for all things, as the Wise Man
said. God meant children to be *children*, not adults in

miniature. Zinzendorf was convinced that children are born to be happy ; so long as they are children they cannot but be happy. To ask them to forgo their birthright, to seek to make them hurry through child-hood, as some would have them do, is altogether wrong.

A little later Zinzendorf produced a catechism for older people. It is not a dogmatic treatise. Though very long it is very simple. Most of the answers indeed consist of short passages of Scripture.

The older he grew the less Zinzendorf cared for formal catechetical teaching of the old-fashioned sort. ' Through it ', he said, ' the child learns to chatter about hundreds of things which he can neither believe nor understand.' To *make* a child learn his catechism, to punish him if he failed to learn it or learned it amiss, as was the custom in those days, was to Zinzendorf little short of infamy. ' To introduce children ', he once said, ' at one and the same time to the cudgel, the rod, and the wounds of Jesus, to punish them for not knowing the details of the Passion, is altogether wrong.'

These, then, are the first two great characteristics of Zinzendorf's theory of religious education. The head must never be allowed to outrun the heart. Outward compulsion can *never* produce religion.

## HYMNS

' It is an established and well-known fact ', said Zinzendorf in the year before he died, ' that our hymns provide the best method for inculcating religious truths and for conserving those in the heart.' ' According to our way of singing ', says a Moravian writer, ' the materials of instruction are both presented and reviewed through song. Hence we do not sing through entire hymns of ten to twenty verses, but rather separate stanzas or half-stanzas from as many hymns as the sequence of thought of the subject matter requires.'

The young Moravian had two text-books, the Bible and his hymn-book. His religious teaching largely consisted of a simple exposition of some portion of Scripture, interspersed with antiphons and responses taken from hymns. This, to use Zinzendorf's favourite phrase, was the ' liturgical method ' of giving religious education. The hymns sung at Herrnhut were almost entirely Christo-centric or expressions of feelings which love of Christ awakens in the heart. There were a great many festival services (Zinzendorf believed that monotony is bad for the adult and fatal for the child), and many services at which there was nothing but hymn singing of this antiphonal kind. The Moravians have made more use of the hymn as a means of instruction than any other body of Christians. This is entirely due to Zinzendorf.

## THE LITTLE BIBLE

Two further points are worth attention. Zinzendorf believed that there are many passages in the Bible which refer almost exclusively to Jews and are, therefore, of little interest or concern to Christian children. In view of this he shortened the Bible. What is more, over a hundred years before the Moffatts and the Weizsäckers began to turn the Bible into ' modern speech ' Zinzendorf had done the same thing. It is true that he did not finish his task ; none the less he saw clearly that there is a place in religious education for a shortened Bible, and a Bible translated into the idiom of contemporary speech.

## KINDER-LOOSUNGEN

Each year Zinzendorf carefully selected 365 verses from Scripture. (These were sometimes printed as a booklet.) Each day one of these verses was chosen by lot (Los : hence the name Loosungen). This was the motto for the day. The motto was the theme, the centre round which revolved the reading, talking, singing of that particular day.

## WALKING WITH JESUS (UMGANG MIT CHRISTUS)

We must now turn our attention to that in Zinzendorf's teaching which is at once most characteristic, and at the same time most difficult to explain.

He set out, in his educational work, from Francke's standpoint. When he opened his orphanage he at first followed the Halle method of dividing the children in his dormitories into three classes : The Dead, The Awakened, The Converted. For a time he did his utmost to see that children were ' converted '. He preached to them, prayed with them, talked with them one by one about their soul's salvation. In course of time, however, he ceased to believe in the permanent value of these very youthful ' conversions '. He ceased to desire them, and adopted an entirely different method, based on a completely different point of view.

This is not a book on divinity ; we cannot discuss, as perhaps we ought, the meaning of ' original sin ', ' baptism ', ' conversion '. Suffice it to say that Zinzendorf came to believe that there was no need for a child born in a Christian home[1] to wander into the ' far country ' or to experience that sense of misery and

---

[1] Zinzendorf laid great stress on 1 Cor. vii. 14.

contrition which was demanded by Francke and other
Pietists from all who passed from death unto life.
Of the unknown God, said Zinzendorf, we can know
nothing. All that we can know of Him is that which
is revealed in the God-Man, Jesus Christ. The whole
purpose therefore of Zinzendorf's teaching is to make
the child see Christ ' as clearly as he can see a house ',
to dwell in His presence continually, to live with Him
and for Him at every moment of his life. This ' walking
with Christ ' is the very heart and soul of religious
education. It is not something purely ' other-worldly ' ;
it is a way of life which may be lived in the most
concrete possible form. It embraces every conceivable
activity, and is suffused throughout with joy.

Thus Zinzendorf becomes the champion of freedom,
the first great champion of freedom in the realm of
religious education. The old have no right, he insists,
to impose their own particular opinions upon the
young ; parents have no right to demand that their
particular form of religious experience shall be repeated
in identical form in their children. (This is where he
broke away from Francke.) So long as the child ' walks
with Christ ' he may be safely left to himself, for he
is being taught at every moment of his life by the best
of all teachers, Christ's Holy Spirit.

The function of the teacher, therefore, is to suggest,
rather than to inform in a purely dogmatic way. For
the central point in teaching is not dogma, it is the
child himself. We have to pray to be made like children ;
they have no need to become like us. They emerge
from the baptismal font as ' anointed princes ' and are
to be treated as such. Even in questions of purely
' secular ' education the child must be given the utmost

freedom. The syllabus, the time table, are to be made for him ; he is not to be fitted into them.

Zinzendorf, then, is in all educational matters, an apostle of freedom, a convinced believer in individualism. Self-activity, directed by the Holy Spirit, in a religious environment, is the best form of religious education. That which is inherent in the child, and, with the help of Christ—Who constantly speaks to his heart—develops from the child, not something imparted to the child in dogmatic form by older people, is the basis of all true religious education.

The danger that lies in this emphasis on individual development, is that it may end in egoism. Zinzendorf felt that he had overcome this difficulty. In the very nature of things, he maintained, fellowship with Christ involves service of one's neighbour. It is impossible to be a Christian and an egoist at one and the same time. Those who love Christ know that they are not their own they exist to carry out their Father's will.

## THE CHOIRS

We must now consider that which Zinzendorf regarded as the most characteristic and the most important feature in his system of religious education. He divided the whole community into groups according to age, sex, ' condition ' (i.e. as to whether they were married or unmarried). For the whole community education was a process that never ceased. By this method he sought to give each individual that particular kind of education required to meet the varied needs of his particular age and circumstances. Each ' choir ' had its own ideal, its own regular meetings, its own litanies, its own special festivals, days of covenanting and so forth.

Parents, for instance, were organized into one group (Ehe-Chor) and received instruction in such matters as concerned them. They heard addresses on the Christian ideal of marriage, the duties and privileges of parents, the proper method of conducting a Christian home, the right way of training children. Zinzendorf himself had been peculiarly fortunate in having been brought up by a woman who, whilst believing in allowing the utmost freedom, gave no sign of weak indulgence. ' Parents ', he said, ' who become the slaves of their children's whims turn them into little devils.' He himself was most happily married and, a hundred years before the English father, had abandoned the Roman attitude (*patriapotestas*), and made himself the friend and confidant of his own children, who were allowed the widest liberty.

As against the older fashioned type of Moravian, who was often suspicious of married love, and was prone to look upon sexual attraction as a moral evil, Zinzendorf expressly taught that ' children are begotten and born only unto the Lord, as in His Presence '. Few men have had a nobler view of married life and of the sanctity of the home than Zinzendorf.

There were ten other choirs. One for infants in arms (Zinzendorf had wonderful skill in handling babies), one for the little children, one for boys and one for girls, one for the bigger boys and one for the bigger girls, one for young men, one for young women, one for widowers and one for widows. It is impossible to deal with each of these choirs in detail. Two important facts, however, deserve attention.

Zinzendorf presented the boy Jesus to the child as his ideal. All the teaching given in the Junior Choirs was concentrated on this. Jesus was once a child, and the happiness of all children (they were born to be happy) lay in thinking about Jesus, in holding constant communion with Jesus, in asking themselves how, had Jesus been a boy in Herrnhut instead of in Galilee, He would have behaved. On this all the teaching, all the litanies, all the hymns, were based. As the boy grew up he was to think of Christ at a corresponding age ; to think of Him, for instance, as the boy who worked in a carpenter's shop. Throughout their early life, children were trained to devote their whole attention to the earthly life of the boy Jesus. They were taught to regard Him as at once their ideal, their invisible friend and companion. All that savoured of legalism, was rigidly excluded. The utmost care was taken to preserve each child against every approach of evil. Otherwise in almost complete freedom their characters were allowed to develop through constant thought of Jesus, through constant intercourse with their loving friend.

The four things that impressed and delighted Zinzendorf, when he looked at children, were their natural happiness, their frankness, their freedom from care, and what, for lack of a better word, we may call their sociability. Yet none knew better than he that this earthly paradise could not last for ever. The boy had to become man.

Until modern psychology made its appearance, it is safe to say that no man had paid more attention to the problems of adolescence than Zinzendorf. He saw the naïveté, the frankness of childhood give place to self-consciousness and a sense of shame. He watched the melancholy, the desire for solitude, the awkwardness, the ever-changing moods. He saw that the natural happiness of childhood was giving place to mysterious longing for what the youth was utterly unable to explain. This, said Zinzendorf, is the most dangerous period in the life of man. It is the time of crisis. Then, if ever, the youth definitely chooses the right or wrong course in life.

How did he deal with this problem ? First of all by tactful suggestion that such a situation must sooner or later arise ; so that the youth was not taken utterly unawares. Second, by urging the boy in all cases of difficulty or distress to consult the ' Kinder-Vater '. At the head of each choir was a carefully chosen leader, whose business it was to win the love and confidence of each child. The ideal Kinder-Vater was so very hard to find that Zinzendorf felt it was far easier to come by the ideal bishop. Finally the boy was reminded that Christ had once been an adolescent, had experienced the same misgivings, the same unhappiness. He had been exposed to the very same temptations and He had vanquished them. Christ knew from personal experience what suffering meant—had He not died upon the Cross ? Those who put their trust in Him would find that their faithful friend would not fail them. At this period of life, we may add, the ideal presented to the adolescent, was the Christian knight sans peur et sans reproche.

It has been said that the contradictions in Luther's character are due to the fact that his mind was a battlefield on which two epochs fought with one another. It has been suggested that the same is true of Zinzendorf. He stands between two eras, between the old ' authoritarian teaching ' and the ' naturalism ' which we associate with Rousseau (whose *Emile* appeared a year after Zinzendorf's death). Shortly before his death he expressed the conviction that the religious education given at Herrnhut was superior to any other ; ' a great leap forward ' had been made, the methods which had obtained for 150 years were left behind. Not through speculation but through personal experience in dealing with children, he had found a better way.

It may be that Zinzendorf's method in other hands—the same holds good of Arnold—will not yield equally satisfactory results : that a form of education well suited to the needs of a small, exceptionally devout, community is not applicable to the varied schools of a great country like our own. Zinzendorf's theory and Zinzendorf's method may be equally defective, yet no teacher of religion can fail to profit by being brought into contact with one who, despite his many weaknesses, has much to teach. He reverenced children, he loved children as few have done. He was one of themselves : they knew it and they loved him. Few men—*none* known to the present writer—have equalled him in the art of addressing children, in making the Bible a living thing for children, in touching the hearts of children. Nor has any rivalled him in the yet more difficult task of dealing with the adolescent.

# CHAPTER VIII

## *Johann Heinrich Pestalozzi (1746-1827)*

'ALL for others : nothing for himself.' The epitaph inscribed on Pestalozzi's monument is well deserved. In nobility of character his only rival in the whole history of education is Comenius. Throughout a long life he was a social reformer who regarded education as the chief means by which the changes he so ardently desired might be brought about. A great teacher—'one of the world's greatest pioneer educationists '—who introduced new methods and influenced both Herbart and Froebel, he has perhaps made a deeper impression, direct and indirect, on the modern school than any other. A profoundly religious man, who said in his first published book that ' Man's relationship to God is the nearest of all his relationships ', he was convinced that education ' must be essentially religious '. ' Faith in God ', he said, ' is graven in man's nature ; as is the sense of right and wrong indestructible, so is this, *the unchangeable foundation of human education*, to be found in the innermost recesses of his nature.' He is, as he deserves to be, the central figure in this book. Yet he is the most difficult person to deal with : for (1) it is impossible to understand Pestalozzi's work without knowing the story of his life, and we have no room for biography. (2) In the eighteen volumes which he left behind there is no *systematic* presentation of his educational views, and these in turn are based on a concept—*Anschauung*—for which there is no equivalent in English. (3) It is no easy matter to understand the sense in which he used the word ' religion '. His views varied. In early life he was a devout believer, in later years his early faith seems to have returned ; but in his ' middle period ' he described himself as *ungläubig*, that is to say a ' freethinker ', who adopted a critical, nay, even a sceptical attitude, to certain essential elements of the Christian faith.

The two first difficulties may be easily overcome. In the *Cyclopaedia of Education*[1] Professor Holman has given an adequate account of Pestalozzi's life and a masterly exposition of his educational principles. As it is impossible to improve upon Holman's work we take the liberty of copying out the six principles to which he reduces Pestalozzi's educational theory.

(1) ' Education must be essentially religious.'

(2) ' Education must develop man as a whole.'

(3) ' Education must guide and stimulate self-activity.'

(4) ' All education must be based on intuition and exercise.' (This is the celebrated doctrine of *Anschauung*.)

(5) ' Education must observe a right graduation and progression in development.'

(6) ' Education must foster the growth of knowledge through the development of ideas.'

From these six principles, says Holman, five rules may be deduced. These he states as follows :

(1) ' An all-round training must be given.'

(2) ' All possible liberty must be allowed to the learner. The nature of the child must determine all the details of his education.'

(3) ' Work is more important than words. Man is

[1] New York, 1911 (Macmillans).

more truly educated through what he does than through what he learns.'

(4) 'The method of learning must primarily be analytic. We put our children on the road which the discoverer of the subject himself took and had to take.'

(5) 'Realities must come before symbolism in education. Elementary education must aim at establishing connexions between the child and the realities of his actual life.'

## Religious Education

At least twelve writers have discussed and criticized Pestalozzi's views on this subject. Nearly all of them, however, have written in German (some of their books are not to be met with in England) and demand a knowledge of philosophy and theology which the average reader cannot be expected to possess. In the following pages, therefore, we shall begin by giving an account of what Pestalozzi said on the subject, together with some of the chief criticisms that have been passed upon his views. We shall then proceed to describe, as well as we can, his own procedure when in charge of a school. This is no easy matter. We shall end with a short criticism based on the assumption that any man so pervaded by the spirit of the ' enlightenment ' as Pestalozzi was is thereby unfitted to understand some of the most important elements in the Christian religion.

*How Gertrude teaches her children.*

The classic account of Pestalozzi's views on religious education is to be found in the closing chapters of his immortal work *How Gertrude teaches her children.* Pestalozzi begins with a question. ' How is it ', he asks,

' that the conception of God originates in my mind ? How do I come to believe in Him, to trust Him and to love Him ? ' ' I soon see ', he answers, ' that the feelings of love, trust, gratitude and readiness to obey, must be developed in me before I can apply them to God. I must love men, trust men, thank men, and obey men before I can aspire to love, thank, trust and obey God.' ' For whosoever loveth not his brother whom he hath seen, how can he love God, whom he hath not seen ? '

But how do I learn to love my fellow-men ? ' All love ', says Pestalozzi, ' arises from the relationship that exists between the infant and its mother.' The mother satisfies her child's physical needs, and out of the sense of satisfaction comes gratitude to the giver. The mother soothes her frightened child, and out of the sense of protection comes trust in his protector. In earliest infancy the impatient child cries for his mother's breast. She tends him when she is ready to do so, not when she first hears his cry. From this experience, often repeated, come the germs of patience and obedience. Obedience and love, gratitude and confidence, when blended together result in the first germ of conscience. The child feels that it is ' wrong ' to struggle against the mother who loves him ; the child learns that the mother is not in the world merely, perhaps not even primarily, for his sake. Out of these dim feelings arises the first vague sense of right and wrong.

All this, however, takes place in the realm of instinct. The child does not think or reason, he merely feels. At this stage love and trust are merely the instinctive germs out of which *real* love and trust develop. Gradually, however, the child *does* learn to love and trust his mother, to be grateful to his mother, to obey his mother. To be capable of loving, trusting, obeying is inherent in the child as a human being. These powers are developed by exercise. Thus instinct is spiritualized, or to put the same thing in another way, instinct reveals itself as spiritual. Henceforward it is the task of the mother to extend the sphere in which these moral powers are exercised. The child sees her kiss other children and thus learns the meaning of ' brotherly love '. He learns to love and trust his brothers, his sisters, and other men. Trusting solely in his mother's judgement, relying utterly on her word, he extends his love, his trust, to people whom he has not seen, and to God. Long before he has heard such expressions, let alone acquired the power of understanding them, he has seen revealed in the *actions* of his mother Christian love and faith. All this is *bound to happen* if only the mother is content to be guided by instinct. Just as it is instinct which teaches her to satisfy her child's needs, so it is ordained of God that by obeying instinct she shall implant the germs of religion and morality in the heart of her child. ' When the mother says to the child, I have a Father in Heaven, from whom comes all the good that you and I possess, the child believes, on the strength of his mother's statement, in his Heavenly Father ; and when the mother prays, and reads the Bible, and believes, the child prays along with his mother to his Father in Heaven ; believes in the love of Him whose activities he has already seen in his mother.' Thus he passes from merely instinctive physical love to ' human ' love, to real Christian love.

In order to understand all this, four things must be borne in mind :

(*a*) In the first period of the child's life there is no

need for words. Feeling is his only guide ; his mother is to him the world.

(*b*) In the second period, during which the child's love, trust and obedience are directed to a wider circle, he needs words. He talks because he has to talk. He does things with his hands, he cannot help it. He walks, he has to walk. Throughout this period he sees his mother pray and read the Bible. She says grace when they sit down to table. He sees that Sunday is not as other days. He sees his mother do deeds of charity.

(*c*) But a time comes when he no longer feels utterly dependent upon his mother. He plays with other children. He learns to trust his own powers. This, says Pestalozzi, is when the testing time comes. Either the child turns from his mother to throw himself into the arms of a ' fallen world ', the embodiment of selfishness and passion, ceases to trust, to obey, to love his mother, becomes rebellious, selfish, self-confident ; or the instinctive feelings of love, trust, gratitude and obedience, which once centred on his mother, are consciously transferred to his neighbours and to God.

(*d*) The sphere in which this conflict takes place is the home. This is the child's world, in which love, trust, gratitude, unselfishness, service, are developed. In this little world, head, heart, and hand are trained pari passu. The mother deliberately sets herself to train her child by arranging his life in such a way that he shall have suitable objects on which to exercise his powers of head, heart and hand. Religion is presented to him in the life his mother leads ; Ethics in the demands made on him in the home, to deny himself, to think of others and to serve others. His education consists not in talk *about* God and virtue, but in seeing his mother talk *with* God and in her life striving to do the will of God. It is love, gratitude, trust which differentiates man from the beast. The young animal speedily becomes independent of his parents ; has no further need for love, gratitude or trust, for conscience or obedience. But man's very nature consists of love, gratitude, trust ; without these he ceases to be man. Therefore the three aspects of his life must be developed in harmony. He must feel, he must think, he must act. In all this the essential guide must be love ; at first in the home, later on in that extension of the home which we call the school. Neither in home nor in school can moral education be given (and all true education is moral) if hand and heart be forgotten. For education is something far richer than ' instruction '. It is the development of personality, development, which automatically takes place in the home, where the child through living, through working, through learning to extend affections and activities, *grows*.

According to Pestalozzi there are two principles that underlie all moral training. The first is continuity. (*a*) ' The earliest instruction given to the child ', he says, ' must never be an appeal to his reason ; it must concern his senses, his feelings. It is his mother's affair.' (*b*) ' It must move very slowly from the realm of sense to the realm of judgement. It must remain for a long time a concern of the heart, before it is handed over to the intellect. It must long remain a woman's duty, before it is taken over by a man.'

The second principle is the ' perfection of others '. Man is not placed in this world for his own sake ; only through perfecting his fellow men does he become perfect.

In one passage Pestalozzi says, ' The God of my brain is a mere chimera, an idol. To worship Him is ruin. The God of my heart is my God.' For the child, mother and obedience, God and duty, are one and the same. ' The human heart demands and creates a personified sublime type which it can love, obey, trust and adore. His will is holy : He is the soul of the spiritual world.' The aim of all education, therefore, is to ' fit a human being to use in the freest and fullest way all the powers implanted in him by the Creator, to become a perfect man so that, in whatever station of life to which he may be called, he shall be an instrument of that all-wise and almighty Power that has called him into life.'

Critics of the views expressed in *How Gertrude teaches her children* may be divided into two groups : there are those who find fault with his psychology ; there are those who condemn his theology.

As representative of the first group we may take a man called Niemeyer, at first an ardent disciple, later a severe critic. According to this writer, Pestalozzi asks of the average mother what she is utterly unable to give. ' I live in a world ', said Pestalozzi himself in his *Journal for Education*, ' in which I seek far and wide in vain for such fathers and mothers.' It is the woman who rears the child rather than the woman who bore him to whom the child is attached. To rear a child a woman needs a good deal more than instinct : she needs intelligence and what may be termed ' pedagogic virtuosity '. It is absurd to say that maternal care inevitably awakens love and gratitude. ' A dead mother is forgotten on the second day.' Children are the greatest egoists ; only when they grow up do they learn to realize the meaning of a mother's love. Finally, though love, trust, gratitude may be termed the elements of religion, since the relation of child to parent is at the best symbol of man's relation to God, yet morality is based on a sense of right and duty, on self-conquest, on the subjection of inclination to reason.

What we may call the ' theological ' critics complain that in *How Gertrude teaches her children* the name of Christ does not once occur, that Pestalozzi says very little (anywhere) about Christ's teaching, that instead of being a mediator between her child and God the mother requires a mediator for herself, that religion cannot be explained as the product of a purely human relationship, that in a word it is impossible to base either ethics or religion on the relationship between mother and child.

## PESTALOZZI'S OWN PRACTICE

During his lifetime it was often said that Pestalozzi gave no ' religious instruction ' in the various schools with which he was connected. How far this charge is true is a very difficult matter to determine. On two points we can be absolutely certain. He was convinced that the proper teacher of religion was the parent (especially the mother). From *Leonard and Gertrude* we discover that the good mother not only reads the Bible to her children, prays with them, observes the Sabbath ; but that every Saturday night she holds a systematic investigation of conscience. She asks each child what he has done during the week, praises him for that which she admires in his conduct, points out the faults that require amendment. In other words, in her own way, she plays the part of the ' Spiritual Director ' of the Roman Catholic Church. In the second place he was strongly opposed to two practices which were almost universal in his time. (*a*) He felt that to make the Bible the child's first ' reader ' was fundamentally wrong. (*b*) He was equally certain that to make a child learn the catechism by heart and repeat it like a parrot could yield only evil results. ' Catechism about abstract ideas ', he said, ' excepting the advantage of separating words and subjects into analytic forms, is nothing in itself but a parrot-like repetition of unintelligible sounds.' ' I have been bold ', he says in another place, ' to say before now that God hates stupidity, hypocrisy and lip-service, and that we should teach children to think, feel and act rightly, and lead them to enjoy the blessings of faith and love that are natural to them, before we make them commit various points of dogma and theological controversy to memory as an intellectual and spiritual exercise.'

It was this deliberate neglect of the catechism which led to so much criticism ; for Pestalozzi gave religious guidance to his pupils that was entirely novel. So far we have spoken as though all his pupils were ' day-boys ' : as a matter of fact many of them were boarders. Two of these boarders have given interesting accounts of their experience. Each refers to the fact that every morning before breakfast Pestalozzi delivered a ' discourse ', sometimes based on a text of Scripture, sometimes on a verse from some familiar hymn, sometimes on a moral duty. Then too, like Gertrude, Pestalozzi gave spiritual guidance, sometimes to

individuals, more often to small groups. In addition
there were prayers at the beginning and end of the day.
Though his enemies maintained that there was *no*
Bible reading in Pestalozzi's school, there *was* Bible
reading. Every Friday, for instance, the story of the
Passion was read. At the same time it is true to say that
there was far less Bible reading in Pestalozzi's school
than in any other.

Pestalozzi always maintained that the whole of his
curriculum was religious ; for it was based on the
effort to cultivate heart and mind, the one directed to
love, the other to truth, and that love and truth are
but two different names for God.

Besides all this, however, there was a certain amount
of religious instruction. (1) In the two lower classes
children were asked to tell what they felt to be
' elevated ' (etwas Höheres) in their own lives, in the
lives of their neighbours, in the world of Nature. This
provided the basis for elementary instruction in
religion. It was, of course, of a purely subjective
character. (2) In the next stage religion was depicted
in a more *objective* way, as something which revealed
itself in truth, love, nature, the life of man. From
historic facts of the Bible children were shown how
' Man attained to objective knowledge of God '.
(3) In the third stage the life of Christ, from the cradle
to the tomb, was dealt with in an ' historico-psycho-
logical ' way. This was followed by treatment of the
' ethico-religious doctrines of the Gospel, especially as
these were manifested in biblical accounts of life in the
Christian Church. (All this for the benefit of those who
were being prepared for confirmation.) Later on elder
pupils received a special kind of religious instruction

which was described as being 'partly philosophical, partly historical, in character.'

No one can pretend that this syllabus of religious education is a good one. In some ways it is an exceedingly bad one. In closing, therefore, we may ask why this should have been the case.

First of all, let us remember that Pestalozzi's whole life was a protest against the schools of his time.[1] In most villages the school was kept by a cobbler or a tailor. Often he taught in his own cottage. In nearly every instance he was an ignorant man. He did his work in a purely mechanical way and was intensely conservative. He refused to introduce any innovation. In no respect was he more bigoted and conservative than when he dealt with religion. His theological opinions, tenaciously held, but seldom understood, were rigidly orthodox. They were a legacy which had come down to him from the bitter and protracted struggle between Catholic and Protestant. In almost every school punishment was severe. ' The punishments of the teacher ', says Diesterweg, ' exceeded those of a prison.' One afternoon, for instance, Luther was ' beaten on his back ' fifteen times. In opposition to all this, Pestalozzi conceived of a very different method of training children. Perhaps we shall understand his ideas best if we think of the sort of training a troop of Boy Scouts receives. The Scout Master begins by asking himself what boys care for. He soon discovers that they like to do things, to make things, to have adventures, to sleep under canvas and to sit around a camp fire as their ancestors did before them. This and much else the wise Scoutmaster knows, and it is this he turns to

[1] See Paulsen, op. cit., p. 141.

advantage. Physical exercise in healthy conditions
develops the body, though the Scout may hear nothing
of physiology or anatomy. Mental powers are developed,
hand and eye are trained, although no reference be
made either to books or to psychology. Character is
disciplined. Loyalty to leader and to comrades, service,
fellowship, unselfishness, obedience and the like are
cultivated, even if there be little explicit reference
either to ethics or theology. In other words we live
before we reflect on life. So it is in all things. So too,
said Pestalozzi, it is in regard to religion. A boy must
experience religion, must *live* religion, before it is worth
while talking to him *about* religion. Theology, even of
the simplest kind, must follow, it can never precede
religious experience. That is the greatest contribution
which Pestalozzi made to the theory of religious
education. He discovered a new *Method*.

When we turn, however, to his interpretation of
religion it is a very different matter.[1] Here he was not
a pioneer. This we may say with safety, even though
we may find it impossible to determine what he meant
by religion. As we have already pointed out, his views
were different at different periods of his life. The
present writer, after giving the matter prolonged
consideration, is not convinced that during the most
important period of his life Pestalozzi interpreted
religion in a Christian sense. The long fight between
Catholic and Protestant, between one form of
Protestantism and another, which marks the sixteenth
and seventeenth centuries ended in rationalism.
Eighteenth century rationalism assumed different

[1] Nicolay (W. O.) : Pestalozzi's Stellung zu Religion und Religions-
unterricht (1920).

forms in different countries ; in England the Deist, in France the Philosopher, in Germany the Enlightened. Yet there was a strong family resemblance between them all. These men asked for a ' reasonable ' religion, free from miracle and superstition. They had little interest in the ' world to come ' ; they felt that, as man's destiny is decided in this world, his main concern is *here*. For them the atoning death on Calvary was of far less moment than the Sermon on the Mount, for to them Christ was essentially a prophet. One religion, so long as it worked well, was as good as another. Indeed, in the last resort there was but one religion, the religion of all sensible men. To ritual, dogma, the ' visible Church ', such men attached little or no importance. Moral conduct was the one thing needful ; religion a private affair between two persons, Man and his Maker. Such a form of religion, marred as it is by the almost complete identification of religion with ethics, shallow rationalism, suspicion of the supernatural, inability to give a satisfactory account either of the Person of Christ or of the Church which He founded, is hardly calculated to make strong appeal. It is too simple to be true ; too cold to be effective. It does indeed get rid of the superstition and bigotry which mar so many other forms of religion, but in so doing it throws away the baby with the bath water. Two forces influenced Pestalozzi ; one was Rousseau, the other, for many years, this type of religion.

For that reason, then, we may say that, if we compare the teacher of religion to a gardener who tends the plants in the Lord's garden, there is no greater than Pestalozzi, who in love and reverence for children is only equalled by Zinzendorf. In *Method* he is supreme amongst those who have won fame as religious teachers. But if we compare the teacher to a wise steward who brings out of his treasure things new and old, who hands out to the rising generation, so far as they are fitted to receive it, the richest spiritual treasures of the past, then Pestalozzi, despite his nobility of character and his genius as a teacher—unequalled as we believe before or since—is sadly disappointing. He has nothing new to tell us about religion, and what he has to tell is so cold and lifeless that in weaker hands it is of little worth.

# CHAPTER IX

## *The Philosophy of Religious Education*
## *Friedrich Daniel Ernst Schleiermacher (1768-1834)*

THE problem of religious education, as we have so
often said, is two-fold, ' What is religion ? '
' How is it to be taught ? ' To the second question the
best answer is given by Pestalozzi ; to the first by
Schleiermacher. Of the distinguished men who figure
in this book, he is fitted, as no other is, alike by ability
and experience, by temperament and training, to deal
with it. ' He is the greatest teacher ', said one schoolmaster, ' the world has ever seen since Socrates.' ' He
inaugurates a new era,' said a distinguished colleague.
' He is the one really great theologian of the nineteenth
century,' says his severest critic.[1] ' His contribution to
the problem of religious education ', says a Canadian
writer, 'is the most significant that has yet been made.'[2]
He is perhaps the greatest man who has dealt with the
fundamental problems that lie at the root of education
since Plato.[3]

Three forces combined to form his character and to
determine his opinions :

---

[1] Emil Brunner : *Die Mystik und das Wort*, 2nd Ed. (1928), p. 6.
[2] A. R. Osborn : *Schleiermacher and Religious Education.*
[3] Eitle's article in K. Schmid : *Geschichte der Erziehung* Stuttgart,
5 vols. (1884-1902) (Vol. 4, pt. 2) is almost dithyrambic. But others
speak in superlatives. Thus Dilthey : ' No thinker since Socrates ;
not even Spinoza or Kant has exercised such a remarkable influence
on his environment.'

(1) The religious influence of a Moravian school.
(2) A thorough training in philosophy, without which no theology worthy of the name can be produced.
(3) The Romantic movement.

(1) Son of a devout Army chaplain, who, when he had to leave home with his regiment, sent his son to a Moravian school, Schleiermacher spent his early years under strong religious influence. Despite a period of doubt, which came when he was 18, he could never remember a time in which religion had not been the most real and important thing in his life.

(2) When he went to the university, the influence of Kant was at its height. Profoundly influenced as he was by the critical philosophy, Schleiermacher never believed that Kant had solved the problem of how the individual is related to the universe. He had an even greater teacher, Plato, whose works he subsequently translated so well that his version became a classic.

(3) Rationalism was dead and all Europe hailed the dawn of a better day.

> Bliss was it in that dawn to be alive
> But to be young was very heaven.

So cried Wordsworth, who with Scott (and, as some would add, the ' Oxford Movement ') is the greatest representative of romanticism in this country. Schleiermacher was intimately associated with the leaders of the romantic movement in Germany. In those early days he felt as Wordsworth felt. ' I shall never lose my keen zest for life; I pledge myself to an eternal youth.' ' The pulse of my inner life will beat with vigour until death.' Aglow with life and ardour, filled with noble dreams and lofty visions, he was asked by a fellow romantic to write a book. The *Reden* (addresses on religion to its cultured despisers) was the result. It is one of the greatest apologias ever written, from the days of Justin Martyr to the days of Newman. It is perhaps unequalled as a brilliant account in limited space (it consists of but five chapters) of what religion in its inmost essence really is.

With the years that followed, and the work he did as a patriot, we have no space to deal ; suffice it to say that from the time when he returned to Berlin in 1810 until he died in 1834 he was the greatest figure in the city. He was renowned as a great preacher. 'His church was a big family ; his family a little church.' A catechist to whom all the élite sent their children to be prepared for confirmation—Bismarck went, though he did not relish the experience—he was at the same time the most powerful influence in the University, admired by colleagues, adored by students.

Of the thirty-one volumes which (apart from five volumes of letters and five volumes of Plato) formed his ' works ', five-sixths are records of sermons, lectures and addresses. We are only concerned with three. One of these consists of notes which students made of three sets of lectures. It is called

### ' THE PEDAGOGICS '.

This book,[1] which deals with education in general, has been described as a series of monographs on the fundamental problems that lie at the root of education. Perhaps it is better to regard it as a rough outline of a

---

[1] ' The most profound, the most fundamental, the most comprehensive and luminous treatment which Pedagogics has yet received ' (Baur).

philosophy of education. Here we can only indicate, in the briefest possible way, some of the chief questions with which it deals.

To Schleiermacher, education is an art which deals with one department of ethics. No theory of education can be satisfactory which is not based on a theory of the Good, for it is the purpose of education to produce a moral being who will eventually identify himself with each of the four great forms of human fellowship—the State, the Church, the knowledge which men possess and share, the intercourse they have with one another through commerce and social life. But education is also connected with politics. One must have a theory of the State, must make up one's mind how far the individual has inalienable rights, how far he has to yield to external compulsion. Finally all education must be based on anthropology ; that is to say the teacher must have some theory as to what man is, and how far one person differs, and should be allowed to differ, from another.

Pedagogy must determine : when education begins and when it ends ; how educational activities are to be distributed amongst Family, Church and State ; how far education should develop and how far repress innate qualities ; how far the pupil is to be trained merely to fit into society as it exists ; how far his education is intended to fit him to know and aim at a better state than society has yet attained. Pedagogy has to determine how far education should be democratic, how far aristocratic ; that is to say whether the privileged should remain privileged, or whether it is advisable to open every career to talent. A right theory of education has to settle how far the child is to be nationalist, how

far cosmopolitan, in his sympathies ; how far the child
is to be 'protected' from external influence of an
unfavourable kind ; how far made strong by knowing
what the external world is really like.

Many other weighty matters are discussed. Of these
we can only mention two. (1) All education looks
forward. The child will some day be a man and he must
be prepared for manhood. Yet the process of education
must yield immediate satisfaction at every stage.
Lessons and Play—each equally necessary—must at
every stage be valued for themselves, not merely as a
preparatory discipline for future life. (2) Just as man
cannot know Absolute Truth, so too there is for him in
this world no Absolute Good. Hence there can never
be any theory of education which is valid for all times
and all places. The nature of the education which the
child receives must be determined in every instance by
the condition of the society of which he is a member.

## RELIGION

We now turn to Schleiermacher's treatment of
religious education. Before we do so, however, we must
attend to what he has to tell us about religion. The
*Christian Faith* (*Glaubenslehre*), in which his maturest
views are expressed, is admitted by all to be the most
important work on theology since Calvin's *Institutes*.
Its position is still unchallenged.

Descartes once said, *Cogito ergo sum* ; existence
and consciousness are inseparable. Schleiermacher
maintains that self-consciousness and consciousness of
our relation to the universe involve each other.
God-consciousness and self-consciousness are inseparable. In other words religion is the most fundamental

thing in man. It is essentially a sense of complete dependence on God. The following five quotations from the *Christian Faith* may serve to make his position clearer.

(1) ' The self-identical essence of piety is this—the consciousness of being absolutely dependent, or, which is the same thing, being in relation with God.'

(2) ' The religious self-consciousness, like every essential element in human nature, leads necessarily in its development to fellowship or communion . . . a Church.'

(3) ' Christianity is a monotheistic faith, belonging to the teleological type of religion, and is essentially distinguished from other such faiths by the fact that in it everything is related to the redemption accomplished by Jesus of Nazareth.'

(4) ' Only through Jesus, and thus only in Christianity, has redemption become the central point of religion. . . . There is no other way of obtaining participation in the Christian communion than through faith in Jesus Christ.'

(5) ' Christian doctrines are accounts of the Christian religious affection set forth in speech.'

Two other features complete the picture. (1) Religion has a validity of its own ; it is not a department of ethics or philosophy. (2) It is communicated from spirit to spirit, not through formal teaching. The following sentences from Oman's translation of the *Reden* will make this clear. (1) ' You need not fear that I shall betake myself to that common device of representing how necessary religion is for maintaining justice and order in the world. . . . Nor shall I say how religion is a faithful friend and useful stay of morality. . . . Piety cannot be an instinct, craving for a mess of metaphysical and ethical crumbs. . . . Religion resigns at once all claims on anything that belongs either to science or morality. . . . Religion is not knowledge and science either of the world or of God. . . . In itself it is an affection, a revelation of the Infinite in the finite, God being seen in it and it in God. (2) Religion is always ' caught '. It can never be ' taught '. ' When religion moves in a man with all its native force, when it carries every faculty of his spirit imperiously along in the stream of its impulse, we expect it to penetrate into the hearts of all who live and breathe within its influence.' Yet religion which lives in the depths of the soul cannot be taught. ' Like everything else then that should ever be present ever active in the human soul, it lies far beyond the domain of teaching and imparting.' It is true that we can communicate opinions and doctrines, ' But we know very well that those things are only the shadows of our religious emotions, and if our pupils do not share our emotions, even though they do understand the thought, they have no possession that can truly repay their toil.' . . . ' Show me one man to whom you have imparted power of judgement, the spirit of observation, feeling for art or morality, then will I pledge myself to teach religion also.'

## RELIGIOUS EDUCATION—THE FAMILY

As we have seen Schleiermacher regarded education as an art, by means of which the child is fitted to take part in the activities of the four great human forms of Fellowship—the Church, the State, the world of knowledge, and social intercourse. For him the germ of all these fellowships is the home. The family is ' the womb of piety '. A child born into a Christian home is from the first surrounded by Christian influence. Mother-love is the source of all love, and no mother needs to be taught her business. To the little child his father is an image of God. From father and mother the child ' catches ' religion. He sees his parents worship. This is his first as it is his most important introduction to religion. Religion is ' presented ' to him in his Mother's love, and in family worship. Love is the sum, the source, the crown, of all true pedagogical activity, of all that parents do to give their children a ' religious education '. The child's curiosity leads him to ask questions about ' family prayers '. The answers given are only bridges across which he eventually reaches ideas. Religious instruction is not tied in any way to particular times and places ; it should only be given when it is asked for. There is no need to trouble the child with the Old Testament. There is no need to take him to church (a children's service is what he needs). There is no need to teach him any creed or formula. To him theological ideas are utterly unreal. In any teaching it is essential to begin with Christ. When conscience wakens and he feels a sense of wrong, then he must be told of the Redeemer.

The home is the germ of the Church ; it is also the germ of the State. It is true that the Law gives no strength to any man to do that which is right. At the same time there can be no education without discipline. In common speech we identify discipline with punishment. As a matter of fact the two are entirely distinct. There is no need to reproduce Schleiermacher's teaching on this point at length ; it is clearly expounded in his sermons. ' Discipline ', he says, ' aims by steady exercise to control and regulate the child's emotions, to subdue all the lower instincts of nature under the rule of the higher, imparts a salutary knowledge of the power of the will and gives an earnest of liberty and internal order.'

Discipline deals with every activity of the child. It forbids and allows. It regulates children's friendships, and games, as well as their instruction and regular work. But it has limits. There is something it can do, something far greater which it cannot do. It is ' the preparing of the way of the Lord, that He may be able to enter ; the adorning of the temple, that He may be able to dwell in it ', but towards the actual entering and indwelling of the Lord, discipline can contribute nothing. ' What have we gained,' he continues, ' if the spirit of God does not actually come and make His abode in our hearts ? '

Religious education, above all in early years, is primarily concerned with the development of a disposition, an attitude in which the religious principle can live, in which a sense of fellowship may be developed. For him in rough outline the Church (and family) is the nurse of religion ; the State (and school) the nurse of morals. There can be no true discipline in the home apart from family worship.

## CONFIRMATION

Although Schleiermacher laid great stress on the lessons learnt in the confirmation class, he yet insisted that the home still remained the chief centre of religious

development. The Church Service, even if it contained
a sermon, was primarily devotional and edifying in
character. The confirmation class was a place of
teaching and learning. Its purpose was to stir the
religious consciousness to prepare confirmands to take
an intelligent interest in worship and to teach them
how to use the Bible. Beneath the dogmatic system
which underlay the Church and the cultus which it
practised, were certain doctrines and concepts. These
the boy had to learn to understand. The three chief
departments of study were the Bible, the Church cultus
and religious poetry. Schleiermacher laid great
emphasis on hymns. He once said that it did not matter
whether those who were training to become teachers
in elementary schools knew anything of modern poetry ;
it was essential that they should know and value the
treasure possessed by the Lutheran Church in her
hymns. The young confirmand was taught Church
history ; but as against all his contemporaries
Schleiermacher insisted that there was no need for
the child to trouble about the Old Testament. Even
the Decalogue did not greatly matter, for all of vital
import in it had been given in a short summary
by Christ. The average catechism Schleiermacher
strongly disliked. Each competent clergyman should
make up a catechism of his own. In any case, all
catechizing must combine two elements ; it must
teach some truth, and it must do this in a ' paranetic '
manner. In other words it must be at one and
the same time instruction and exhortation. It is
obvious that such teaching, though it deliberately
excluded theology, could be given by none save a
trained theologian.

### RELIGION IN THE SCHOOL

Wissmann,[1] who has written by far the best study of Schleiermacher's views on religious education, has proved conclusively that, though he considered the matter for something like forty years, Schleiermacher could never make up his mind as to whether religion should be ' taught ' in school or not. His views varied, but on the whole, whilst he was prepared to admit that there was a place for religious education in the elementary school, he felt that it was entirely out of place in the secondary school. It was for the Home and Church to teach religion, not the school. Indeed he maintained that the idea of giving religious instruction in school was a survival from the time when all schools were clerical institutions. This statement requires modification, yet it is substantially correct.

The schoolmaster is the representative of Law. His mission is to develop ' insight ', to train ' capacities '. His work lies on the circumference of the soul, not at its centre. He must, in the elementary school, train the child's powers of imagination, since these will eventually yield fruit in the sphere of religion and morals. The child should learn to sing, to know Bible stories and stories of the Reformation, since later on he will become a member of the Lutheran Church.

No one can speak with absolute confidence about Schleiermacher's views on religious education in the secondary school.[2] Much depends on a certain document which we cannot discuss here. Yet even if

---

[1] Erwin Wissmann : *Religiös Pädagogik bei Schleiermacher* (1894). But see also Paul Diebow : *Die Pädagogik Schleiermacher's im Lichte seiner und unserer Zeit* (1894).

[2] See Wissmann, op. cit., p. 249 ; pp. 258-65.

he did allow religious instruction of a sort in the upper and lower school he was definitely opposed to it in the middle school. If the teacher prepared boys for confirmation the pastor became a mere examiner ; if the pastor did the work there was no need for the teacher to try to cover the same ground. In school one could tell the story of Christ and His apostles, could show how the Church continued from age to age, could reveal the treasures contained in Scripture, could cultivate imagination and develop a sense of fellowship. All this is a preparation for religion ; but it is *not* religion. That which is born of the flesh is flesh. No man can make another either good or religious. For that a higher power is needed than any possessed by man.

# CHAPTER X

## *Thomas Arnold (1795-1842)*

WHEN Arnold applied for the Headmastership of
Rugby he received a testimonial from the
President of Oriel in which he said that ' if Arnold
were elected, he would change the face of education
all through the Public Schools of England '. He did.

He introduced few changes into the curriculum ; he
was not a great scholar ; he was not a great teacher,
though he could make the Classics live. Dean Stanley
once held out a small notebook to Percival and said,
' I could write down in that little book all that Arnold
ever taught me in the way of instruction.' Even the
prefect system so often associated with his name he
borrowed from Winchester, though he transformed its
spirit. None the less he was a very great headmaster.
' He changed the face of education all through the
Public Schools of England.' ' The dominating idea of
his Rugby life ', says Fitch, ' was that a headmaster is
called of God to make his school a Christian school.
Others thought this ; he preached it like a prophet.'
To him a school was a ' Temple of God '. His lofty
purpose was to weld each boy, each master, into one
organic whole, in which every member was influenced
by every other member, in which each member under
the influence of one pervading corporate spirit made
his own contribution to the common good. In such an

atmosphere and only in such an atmosphere, he held, was it possible to give religious instruction, either in classroom or in pulpit, that was of any use. The most recent discussion of Arnold is much the best that has yet appeared ; it is to be found in E. C. Mack, *Public Schools and British Opinion, 1780-1860*, pp. 236 ff.

Arnold was more than a schoolmaster. He took a lively interest in all that concerned both Church and State. He expressed his opinions freely and forcibly. He made many enemies ; neither ' Evangelical ' nor ' High Churchman ' approved of him. Soon after Stanley's *Life of Arnold* appeared a well-known High Churchman wrote a review of the book.

After saying that it gave him pain to write as he did, he went on to give a trenchant criticism of Arnold, the severest and the most able he has yet received. The root of all Arnold's errors, he said, lay in the fact that he was a ' German ' ; that his ' ethos ' was that of ' genuine religious Germanism '. Few more unfortunate explanations have yet been produced ; the man who offered it had as little understanding of German thought as of Arnold's character.

In quite recent times Lytton Strachey included Arnold in his collection of *Eminent Victorians*. With impish glee Strachey detected weaknesses in certain Victorians which their contemporaries had either overlooked or ignored. Dipping his shafts in malice he sought to find entry through joints in the hero's armour to the person of the hero himself. His view of Arnold was welcomed by the cynical, and by those who prefer amusement, skilfully if somewhat maliciously provided, to respectful treatment of what on the very lowest estimate is the distinguished career of a remarkable man. Those of deeper insight and of more generous heart have given a very different picture of Arnold.

One who felt that he lived in an untoward generation acknowledged the debt he owed his father, ' zealous, beneficent, wise ', who had awakened the slumbering conscience and nerved the feeble arm. Because he had known his father, Matthew Arnold tells us, he found it possible to believe in the existence of other good men.

> Yes ! I believe that there lived
> Others like thee in the past
> . . . Souls temper'd with fire,
> Fervent, heroic and good,
> Helpers and friends of mankind.

To men in sore distress these heroes come—Arnold was one of them—

> Ye, like angels appear,
> Radiant with ardour divine !
> Beacons of hope ye appear,
> Languor is not in your heart,
> Weakness is not in your word,
> Weariness not on your brow.

> Therefore to thee it was given
> Many to save with thyself ;
> And, at the end of thy day.
> O faithful shepherd ! to come,
> Bringing thy sheep in thy hand.

John Percival (Bishop of Hereford)[1] himself a passionate lover of righteousness, and one of Arnold's

---

[1] See Findlay : *Arnold of Rugby*, XV, XX, XXI.

greatest successors at Rugby, has thus described him.
' It is by virtue of great qualities and an intensity and
ardour of spirit which would have made him great in
any sphere, that he was a great teacher. . . . He rises
before us like an inspired prophet, preaching to every
schoolmaster the sacredness of his calling and bidding
him always remember that formation of character is
the primary aim of every good teacher. . . . Arnold
infused a new element into the atmosphere of English
education, an element of untold influence to purify and
stimulate. . . . Every master so inspired (i.e. by
Arnold's influence) will say in his heart, " Here are
those who have been created, not for the life of
sensualism or frivolity or self-seeking or greed, but to
be citizens of the Commonwealth of Christ." '

To understand Arnold we must read the sermons
which he preached in the chapel of Rugby School.
From them we may learn, as from nothing else, what
he understood by religious education, what he thought
about the way in which it should be given.

He was never weary of saying that he who sought to
teach must be well versed in two subjects : that which
he taught, and the character of those to whom he taught
it. Let us follow his own example and let us begin with
his views on boys.

## THE BOY

Many of his pupils came to him when they were
ten or eleven ; most of them left when they were
eighteen. ' I would ', says the shepherd in Shakespeare's
*Winter Tale*, ' there were no age between ten and
three and twenty, or that youth would sleep out the
rest.' To Arnold the years between ten and twenty

were not only the most formative years, they were the
most critical. Innocence lay behind : the moral
strength of manhood was not yet attained. He once
compared a school with the wilderness. Egypt, like
Eden, lay behind, Canaan was not yet entered. The
virtue of the little child, he said, lay in its ' humility ',
or as he preferred to call it, ' teachableness ' ; its faults
were ' ignorance, selfishness, a life lived in the present '.
' The boy, less humble, retained the " ignorance, the
selfishness, the thoughtlessness " of the child.' He asked
his hearers in one sermon, if it were not possible to put
away these childish things, ' to speed the change from
child to man ', ' to grow in love and in thoughtfulness
faster in youth than we now commonly do grow.' To
enable this to be done was, he felt, the specific object
of religious education, and he was convinced that this
purpose could be achieved. In view of this, he insists
over and over again on the need for ' thoughtfulness '.
The readiness of the great majority of men to follow
the example of their neighbours, without asking whither
they are being led, he regarded as one of the greatest
evils of his time. To him this was a form of idolatry ;
human opinion was made a substitute for the will of
God. Until a boy freed himself from slavish subjection
to the herd there was no possibility of moral progress.
The revolt against such subjection was always attended
with pain, and called for courage. It was so easy to do
what everyone else did, so hard to resist the example
of the great majority ; partly because it was more easy
at all times to do evil than good—we are by nature
sinful—partly because of what the French call
' L'esprit de solidarité dans le mal '. In a school evil
influences, unless they be overcome, triumph over the

good. To Arnold's mind the greatest temptation in a boy's life was cowardice ; his greatest need, courage.

Arnold's first object, then, is to explain to the boy what he really is, to point out his faults of character in the clearest possible way. He strips off the tinsel with which evil is wont to adorn herself and shows sin in its naked horror. The portrait which Arnold painted of the average boy, and the portrait of himself which the boy would have painted had he possessed the requisite ability, are very different. Arnold tried to show him not what he looked like to himself, not what he appeared to others, but what he really was, what he looked like in the sight of God.

What he did for the individual he tried to do for the school. It, too, had a character of its own, and this character was defective. In one sermon he quoted a saying, current at the time, to the effect that ' public schools are the nurseries of vice', nor did he altogether disapprove of it. Throughout his stay in Rugby he insisted that the traditions, the practices, of any school must be submitted to the judgement of God. Many faults looked upon as venial by boys are regarded in a very different way by God ; much that is admired in a school is condemned by God. The boy's scale of values is altogether wrong. In Rugby the highest value was set on physical strength, the next on mental ability, the least on moral character. According to Arnold the scale of values should be precisely the reverse. The school as a school must be viewed *sub specie aeternitatis* to see how far its spirit, its customs and traditions are calculated to fit a boy to realize the end for which he was created—eternal life in the presence of God. Religion, he insisted, had much to say with regard to every department of school life. If the school was primarily a place for the development of character, it was in the second place a seat of learning. Its main work was the work done in the classroom. In Arnold's eyes indolence was a cardinal sin. He was at one with Browning in his view of the ' unlit lamp and the ungirt loin ' ; in evil he included what he called ' omitted good '.

Arnold assumed, all too readily, that the Rugby curriculum of his day was the divinely appointed means of mental and moral discipline ; that those who found it utterly distasteful were morally guilty, since what at first was utterly repulsive would through resolute perseverance eventually bring pleasure. In this, of course, he was entirely wrong. But he was right in insisting that for most of us it is easier to be self-indulgent, and to make excuses, than it is to face and conquer difficulty ; that the Christian character can only be acquired by those who perform what at their best they realize to be their duty :

> And tasks in hours of insight willed
> Must be in hours of gloom fulfilled.

In almost every instance this means, in some places, monotony and drudgery. It is idle to suppose that a task imposed by external authority, whether it be human or divine, will be always pleasant ; the very contrary is the case. It is essential to believe that work given by God, or by those whom we regard as His representatives, must be done to the very best of our ability.

Arnold gloried in calling himself a disciple of Aristotle. He did not deal with sin and duty ; he always spoke of sins and duties. He split up general concepts into their constituent parts. It would be tedious to follow him throughout this process. Those who wish to do so must read his sermons ; for the rest it is better that each should analyse these general concepts for himself. The point to notice, however, is that Arnold strove by every means in his power to show a specific number of boys, who lived together in a specific place, who were assailed by specific temptations and were presented with specific opportunities of intellectual, moral and spiritual growth, what they really were, and what they ought to try to become. He did this for the individual ; he tried to do the same thing for the school, that specific society of which all the boys were members, the whole which was in so many ways greater than the sum of its constituent parts.

## THE BIBLE

Arnold insisted on reform ; if the boys were to cease from evil it was essential that they be shown how to learn to do good. To the classics in general and to Aristotle in particular, Arnold attached great value, as we have already seen. He admired certain doctors of the Christian Church—he acknowledged the debt he owed to Butler and to Hooker—yet in the last resort he did not believe that the heathen, however great, could reveal the secrets of eternal life. Dogma he rarely mentions ; to him it was of purely secondary value. He rarely mentions the doctrines of the Church. He asked his boys to read biography, convinced that the devout of all ages and of all sects have much to teach us when on bended knee they address the Father of us all. He invited boys to come to Holy Communion even if they were not confirmed, assuring them that they had no need to fear the taunts of those who suggested that they received the Sacrament not to obtain divine grace but to curry favour with masters, or to lay claim to superior piety which they did not possess. The Sacrament meant much ; yet it meant less to Arnold than it means to many, perhaps most, Churchmen. To him prayer and the Bible were the chief means of grace.

It is, therefore, of some moment to discover the exact way in which Arnold regarded the Bible. His views are set forth not only in many passages of his sermons, but also in an essay which he wrote on the ' Right Interpretation and Understanding of the Scriptures '.

(1) When Arnold came into contact with the ' critical ' treatment of Roman history he was filled with enthusiasm for the work of a great German critic. He bewailed the fact that so few English divines had an adequate knowledge of Hebrew. And it is as certain as any doubtful matter can well be, that had he been acquainted with the critical views of the Old Testament which obtain to-day in almost every circle of Christian society, he would have embraced them. Lacking this clue to the interpretation of Hebrew history, he falls back on the doctrine of *Accommodation.* God, Who might have fully revealed His truth to the men of old, revealed it but in part. The amount of truth they received was conditioned by their state of moral and intellectual progress. It was the childhood of the world and God treated men as children.

(2) The Law is a schoolmaster to bring us unto Christ ; this was a favourite idea with Arnold. There

is something in each of us which prompts us to resist divine commands simply because they are commands. It is easier to disobey God than it is to obey him. The Law, against which we constantly rebel, since it seems to be arbitrary and external, reveals the hold which sin has over each of us. St. Paul tried to keep the Law and because he found he could not do it, sought a Saviour. This lies at the root of much of Arnold's preaching. He assures his boys that they will never really turn to Christ—no matter what they say in hymn or prayer or creed—until they feel the need of Him. Once they discover this, they will find it impossible to leave Him. But till this need is felt all religious words are only words : they are really devoid of meaning. As John the Baptist came to preach repentance, and fitted men to greet the Messiah by telling soldiers to be content with their wages and those who had two coats to give one to those who had none, so God always prepares the human heart to welcome Christ by proclaiming His stern inexorable Law. More than once Arnold told his boys that he longed to preach the Gospel to them ; that he could not do so since they were not ready to receive it. Hence he must continue to talk to them of sin and duty and the Law.

(3) To profit by the message contained in Scripture we must fulfil two conditions. (a) We must take the utmost pains to form a clear conception of the circumstances in which the message was delivered, of the people to whom it was first addressed. (b) We must then examine our own condition with similar care, and thereby learn what the message is intended to convey to us. Arnold condemned those teachers who rest content with quoting St. Paul's words ; he insisted it

was their duty to explain the words, to turn them into English which the boys could understand. When this is done, no divine message contained in Scripture—so far as it is applicable to us—can be readily misunderstood. To discharge this duty it was essential that teachers should employ the same method in interpreting Scripture as they used in understanding and explaining any other book. For mere intellectualism Arnold had nothing but contempt. It was a danger when not controlled by moral purpose. The Bible was written not to present a system of thought on which a man might exercise his subtle wits ; it was written to tell men how to think of God and how to act. Nor yet was it written to fulfil some aesthetic purpose. It is not a sword ' to be gazed on as a child gazes on a soldier's uniform ' ; it is a weapon to be employed in a desperate struggle the issue of which is life or death. To learn how to wield this sword to best advantage, we must make use of all the knowledge which God has given us. ' Hence it is clear ', he says, ' that neither is the Bible alone sufficient to give a complete religious education, nor is it possible to teach history and moral and political philosophy with no reference to the Bible, without giving education that shall be anti-religious. For in the one case, the rule is given without the application, in the other the application is derived from the wrong rule.'

In conclusion we must consider the paradox that the man who did more for religious education than any other Englishman, was firmly persuaded that religion could *not* be taught. Of the sermons which he preached in Rugby Chapel he once said : ' No doubt, the object here is instruction. It is not so much in itself a religious exercise, as a means to enable you to perform religious exercises with understanding and sincerity.' ' Even the Church does not make Christians ', he said on another occasion, ' and therefore he who thinks that to provide schools is to provide education, or that to provide schools where the Bible and Catechism are taught is to provide religious education, will undoubtedly be disappointed when he sees the fruit of his work.' ' Such teaching and such learning ', he continues, ' does not save souls, though it at least gives a man a map of the road which he is going, which will keep him in the right way if he uses it. The map will not make his limbs stronger nor his spirits firmer ; he may be tired or he may be indolent, and it is of no use to him then.' ' Schools ', he continues, ' can indeed instruct.' But to give a man a Christian education is to make him love God as well as to know Him, to make him have faith in Christ as well as to have been taught the facts that He died for our sins and rose again, to make him open his heart eagerly to every impulse of the Holy Spirit, as well as to have been taught the fact, as it is in the Nicene Creed, that He is the Lord and Giver of Spiritual Life. We may show boys the well of living water ; we cannot force them to drink of it.

In saying all this Arnold of course but re-echoes the teaching of men greater than himself. ' I have planted, Apollos watered ; but God gave the increase.' ' The wind bloweth where it listeth, and thou hearest the sound thereof, but canst not tell whence it cometh and whither it goeth : so is everyone that is born of the Spirit.'

This brings us to the very heart of the problem of religious education. Despite all that they have written, the greatest theologians of the past have been unable to explain to us how Faith and Works are connected, how Law and Gospel are related. Yet this is the very question the teacher has to face. What is the relation between Law and Gospel ? With which is a teacher to begin ? How is he to explain to himself, let alone to a child, the precise connexion that exists between Creed and Conduct ? That the Christian life is a ' supernatural ' life most men who take religion seriously are agreed ; for in the last resort the Christian religion turns upon two points, Sin and Redemption.

' If you ask me what wisdom is ', said Arnold in one sermon, ' I point you to the question of the Philippian gaoler.'

Arnold owes his greatness, then, to two facts. In the first place he faced, he did not shirk as most men do, this fundamental problem. He wrestled with it and sought to solve it. For only when this problem is regarded as the permanent background of all our thought in regard to religious education is our thought about religious education of any worth.

In the second place Arnold was, as his son put it, a

soul tempered with fire,
Fervent, heroic, and good.

' Miracles have ceased ', he once exclaimed, ' the prophets are no more.' But Percival was right. He rises before us like an inspired prophet, to remind all who teach that their aim should be to make the school a temple of God, to fit their pupils—' God's scholars ', as he called them—' to become members of the Commonwealth of Christ.'

# CHAPTER XI

## *The Day School*

### A. THE ELEMENTARY SCHOOL

FROM being amongst the most backward in Europe, the English elementary school has become the best in the world. Progress began in 1870 ; during the last thirty years it has become increasingly rapid. The modern school building (costing sometimes as much as from £30,000 to £40,000) ; the text-books used by children in history, geography and literature ; the clinic ; the workshops, the assembly hall, the gymnasium; school plays, school concerts, school excursions, have only to be mentioned to suggest the change. Teachers are now properly trained and adequately paid. No one can enter a modern infant school without feeling the influence of Froebel and Montessori ; no one can listen to a lesson in a Junior school or in a Senior school without recognizing how much the modern teacher has learnt from Pestalozzi and Herbart. Even so great a man as Arnold still followed the old ' authoritarian ' methods : believed that a school was a ' factory in which men are made ' as firmly as did the Jesuits and Comenius, who actually used the phrase (*officina hominum*). All that has been left behind. Nowhere is the influence of the great masters of method more apparent than in the English Elementary school.

Even in the dark days when child-labour was shamefully exploited, when children were sent to factory and mine at the age of eight or even younger, when as yet the State did nothing to educate her children, and most men regarded the lot of the children of the poor with complacency or indifference, certain great-hearted men, who deserve our admiration, resolved that this appalling state of things should cease. Their aims found expression in the National Society, the British and Foreign School Society, and in the first Sunday Schools. The story of their efforts has been often told and need not be recounted here. The literature on the subject is considered in another volume of this series by the present writer. The National Society was founded and supported at great expense by Anglicans who maintained that Religious Education must contain definite doctrine and must be given by a believer. The British and Foreign School Society was mainly supported by Nonconformists who assumed that if God's Word were read His saving message would be received. The Sunday School, which at first combined instruction in secular subjects with religious teaching, confined its energies to religion when national education came into force. The Sunday School has greatly improved. It has now departments for Infants, for Juniors and for Seniors. Preparation classes are held, books on improved method are studied, and lesson notes (some of them admirable) are supplied to teachers. In his *History of Elementary Education* (p. 60). F. Smith says : ' It was through the Sunday School the idea of universal education was first conceived possible.' Be that as it may no one who remembers the unselfish service rendered by generations of Sunday

School teachers—many of them teachers by profession —can withhold a tribute to their loving devotion, and to the personal influence which they exerted on the young. For the most part their work was done in difficult conditions. Neither the buildings in which they taught nor the equipment with which they were provided could bear comparison with those of the modern day school. As regards mere instruction the Sunday School cannot compare with the Day School. In elementary religious education, therefore, the next great step forward will be taken when (1) the length of stay in a training college is extended. As things are, with an already overloaded time table, the student cannot possibly receive the training in religious psychology, the Old Testament, New Testament, Church History, that the use of a modern syllabus requires. (2) When the Sunday School teacher feels able to leave instruction in the facts recorded in the Bible to the Day School teacher, and devotes his attention to preparing his scholars to become intelligent members of the Church to which they belong, by making them acquainted with the story of their own denomination, and of its noblest representatives ; when in a word he emphasizes dogma, Church history, the cultivation of the devotional spirit, as the Day School cannot (and all this may be done in a very simple way)—then the Sunday School will cease to be as it sometimes is, an inferior copy of the Day School. It will then serve a purpose which the Day School cannot serve, and both will gain.

In two respects remarkable progress has been made in the last thirty years. (1) Biblical scholars, teachers and educationists have combined to prepare 'agreed'

Syllabuses.[1] Many such syllabuses have been made. They are steadily improving. One has but to compare the second ' Cambridge Syllabus ' with the first to realize this fact. Closely connected with the syllabus are the various efforts that have been made to provide children with a shortened Bible in an attractive format. These efforts have met with deserved success. Still more important is the change that has taken place in the devotional material supplied to schools. Soon every school will have a hymn-book specially prepared to meet the needs of children. No two men are agreed as to the hymns which such a collection should contain. Tastes differ ; men differ, too, in regard to the age at which children should be introduced to the great classical hymns, as to how long they should be allowed to use the hymns (so much inferior) often heard in the infant school. To the Oxford University Press, which has done so much in this field, the nation owes a debt of gratitude. Then, too, there are books of scriptural lections and collections of prayers.

No one who has watched these changes taking place can fail to rejoice at the steady improvement in religious education given in the Elementary schools.

Perhaps one can realize this best by looking backwards. In 1733 Isaac Watts—the greatest of our hymn

[1] Every syllabus suffers from two defects. (1) It is a compromise. (2) It ignores the backward child. The best individual syllabus yet produced is that of Zange in Baumeister : *Händbuch der Erziehung* (Vol. 3, pp. 1-273). It is influenced by Herbart. The following works are worth consulting : C. Knapp : *The Old Testament : Studies in Teaching and Syllabus*, Vol. I (Murby, 1926). E. T. Campagnac : *Elements of Religion and Religious Education* (1918). N. P. Wood : *Scripture Teaching in Secondary Schools*, Ed. (1912.) See also the Prussian Syllabus on Education, 6th Jan., 1892.

writers, with the possible exception of Charles Wesley—
produced the first children's hymnal. It contains such
verses as these :

(a) There is an Hour when I must die,
     Nor do I know how soon 'twill come ;
     A thousand children young as I,
     Are called by Death to hear their Doom.

(b) There is a dreadful Hell
         And everlasting Pains ;
     There sinners must with Devils dwell
         In Darkness, Fire and Chains.

(c) What if his dreadful Anger burn,
         While I refuse his offer'd Grace.
     And all his Love to Fury turn,
         And strike me dead upon the Place ?

     'Tis dang'rous to provoke a God !
         His Pow'r and Vengeance none can tell ;
     One Stroke of his Almighty Rod
         Shall send young sinners quick to Hell.

To the Hymns certain ' Moral Songs ' are appended.
From these we select the following lines.

         Oft we see a young Beginner
             Practise little pilf'ring Ways,
         Till grown up a harden'd Sinner ;
             Then the Gallows end his Days.

   (In fairness to Watts, it must be remembered that
he was a pioneer.)
   Further light is thrown on the subject by glancing at
the books which children were asked to read. One of
the most celebrated of these books was published in
1671. Its author was the Rev. James Janeway (1636-74),

an Oxford man who was a curate in Hertfordshire. His book is entitled *A token for Children* . . . *Account of the Conversion, holy and exemplary Lives and Joyful Deaths of several young children*. The book was often reprinted (the Religious Tract Society issued an edition in 1865) and was widely read in Germany and America as well as in England. None of the children in the work—there are thirteen of them—lived to be fifteen. Most of them died before they were twelve. Each biography contains a lengthy title : one will suffice to describe the rest.

' Of a child that was much affected with the things of God when he was between two and three years old, with a short account of his life, and death when he was about six years old.'

These stories are followed by eleven rules and a number of ' reflexions '. These in turn are followed by three searching questions. (1) Are you willing to go to Hell to be burned with the devil and his angels ? (2) If other children die, why may not you be sick and die ? (3) How do you know but that you may be the next child that may die ? In *The Fairchild Family* we read that Mr. Fairchild took children to see a man hanged so that they might learn the results of sin, and *The Peep of Day* devotes a chapter to Hell.[1] The writer who reminds us of this tells the following story. ' I'm five years old to-day, Papa,' said a child in 1836. ' Five years nearer your grave, my boy,' replied the father.

The ' authoritarian ' attitude of parents and teachers has disappeared ; they have become the children's *friends*. In his *Discourse on the Education of*

[1] E. E. Kellett : *Religion and Life in the Early Victorian Age* (London, 1938).

*Children and Youth*, Isaac Watts, after insisting that children should be taught ' to govern their inclinations and wishes . . . by the dictates of reason ', bewails the fact that in his time fathers had grown too lax. In his youth, he says, children were not allowed to speak in their father's presence till they were twenty-one. ' Now ', he continues, ' they are made familiar companions of their parents, almost from the very nursery.' ' The last age taught men to think that they were children and treated them as such till they were nearly thirty, but the present gives them leave to fancy themselves complete men and women at twelve or fifteen.'

## B. The Modern Secondary School

There is a close connexion between ethical views, and economic and social conditions. When Isaac Watts described the fate of the ' young pilf'rer ' he was stating a familiar fact. A thief *did* end his days on the gallows. The emphasis on death reflects the high rate of child mortality : many children, perhaps most children born, *did* die. Nor again is it difficult to see some connexion between the views that obtained during the Industrial Revolution and the importance attached by Watts and Wesley to ' industry '.

> Let heathenish boys
> In their pastimes rejoice,
> And be foolishly happy in play ;
> Overstocked if they are,
> We have nothing to spare,
> Not a moment to trifle away.
>                    (WESLEY'S HYMN BOOK)

In the same way the modern High school reflects, as it cannot but reflect, the chaos of the modern world.

The ' modern man ', it has been often said, has lost his way. He knows not ' whence he is sped, nor to what port he sails'. He invents machinery, but this instead of being his servant becomes his master. In a world of plenty, economists know not how the fruits of the earth should be distributed. Neither before nor after the Great War had nations learnt to live at peace one with another. In 1914 Europe learnt that the old faith in automatic progress, in the power of reason to govern life, in happiness and peace as the inevitable outcome of increased wealth and widely diffused culture, was utterly unjustified. Men found that they were living on the crust of a volcano, deep down in the heart of the most civilized are passions as fierce, as diabolic, as any to be met with in a savage. No school can ever march many paces ahead of public opinion.

The education provided in the modern Secondary schools during this chaotic period is generally described as scientific humanism. It is a blend of humanism and science : added to this there is some religious instruction.[1] Now even before the rise of the totalitarian State, it was obvious that this mode of education required to be supplemented from some other source. The school achieved its purpose in developing every side of individual character : it did not always succeed in changing the *moi haïssable* of Pascal into personality. The number of boys who had received a liberal education and who felt impelled, in return for all that they had received, to render service to the community was limited. The chief end of many when they left school was ' to have a good time ' ; only a small minority gave themselves to any form of social service.

[1] See *Reports of Oxford Conference on Church, Community and State* (1937).

The young Nazi who really believed and was prepared to practise the doctrine *dulce et decorum est pro patria mori* had something in him which those reared in the easier conditions of ' the great democracies ' seemed to lack. Only when England's national existence was threatened did men volunteer to serve her at whatever cost. In times of peace, however, the demand for self-sacrifice was apt to be ignored.

If ' moral regeneration ' is to come it cannot come from scientific humanism. When Germany, once utterly broken, was reborn, she turned her back on scientific humanism and adopted an entirely different method. That method, be it right or wrong, had power to evoke enthusiasm and devotion which scientific humanism seemed to lack.

If service of the community is to be rendered continuously, not merely in hours of crisis, it has to be inspired by something very like religion. Something must make an *absolute* claim on the individual if he is to discipline himself. This it will be found, in nearly every instance, has taken the form of a religion ; often a false religion, but always a *religion*. Stoic philosophers dreamed noble dreams of the good life and of the brotherhood of man. It was Christianity that gave men power to transform dreams into reality. *Video meliora proboque* : *deteriora sequor*, was the pathetic cry of a Stoic ; ' I can do all things through Christ which strengtheneth me,' was the exultant shout of a Christian.

It may be said that boys *did* receive ' religious education ' ; to that statement the reply must be a question. In what sense was it religious ? The old Grammar school replaced religion by theology ; in the modern school religion has often been replaced by

' Christian Ethics '. Boys have been taught a good deal about the Sermon on the Mount and the noble code of conduct therein proclaimed. They have not always been taught that Christian ethics cannot be divorced from the Person of Christ. Jesus did not profess to be another Socrates ; He claimed to be the Redeemer of the world. Most Biblical scholars are now agreed that, whatever else the New Testament may be, it is not an ethical treatise. Regarded in that light it is fragmentary and incomplete. It deals with an age and a community or group of communities whose problems were very different from ours. Schleiermacher is profoundly right. Religion has a validity and value of its own. It is something *an sich.*

For ethical purposes we may regard Jesus as a prophet : for religious purposes we must regard Him as a Redeemer. Can the school as a school set Him forth in this light ? That is the fundamental question. Our answer will determine our view of religious education in so far as it is given in school. Schleiermacher, Comenius, Herbart and Arnold are agreed that the school cannot do this. Yet belief in Christ as Redeemer-King is the very essence of the Christian faith. To present Him in any other way is to give a distorted picture. That, then, is the paradox of Religious Education. To view Christ primarily as a Prophet is to distort the New Testament ; to teach boys effectively to regard Him as Redeemer-King seems to lie beyond the scope of any school. If religion be a vitamin which can sustain the human spirit it surely behoves us to ask what it really is and how it is best administered. This is the issue which until yesterday the Secondary school refused to face. Yet even if it be found in the last resort that no school can really ' teach religion ', it is certain that any school can teach a great deal about religion.

(1) To a great extent how far this is done rests with the headmaster. In 1938 a lady was appointed to the headship of a High school. She wrote to an Anglican dignitary to ask his advice when she discovered that no kind of religious teaching had ever been given in that school. On the other hand there are schools in which one of the staff is entrusted with all the religious instruction given in the school.

(2) Nearly every master in a Secondary school has taken an honours degree. He knows his subject and often resents the ' invitation ' to give a lesson on something with which he is imperfectly acquainted. In every school there ought to be one master who knows as much about religion as his colleagues know about French or physics. He must not be a ' careerist ', he must be genuinely religious ; for no man can speak of God as he would of a mathematical problem or a character in history. The religious lesson has a technique of its own. There must be no compulsion, no examinations, no form of punishment.

(3) No school which has a good opening service can fail to teach religion. Worship is the surest way to learn of God. The spirit of the school, when it is of the right order, makes lessons, games, the work of prefects, respect for masters, develop all unconsciously those spiritual muscles without which religion cannot live. Much of the most valuable religious activity of every good school consists in the development of trust, fellowship, loyalty, which when transferred to Christ will be recognized by all as genuine religion.

# POSTSCRIPT

SINCE these pages were written the long expected Spens Report on Secondary Education has appeared. It is one of the most valuable documents of its kind that has been published in recent years, and Chapter V, which deals with the teaching of Scripture, will be welcomed by all who have the cause of religious education at heart. The Report insists, as we have done, that until ' Scripture ' is taught by a specialist it will be taught imperfectly. It rightly suggests that in school the approach to Scripture must be ' historical and objective '. It says, with truth, that such teaching, however essential, is but a part of religious education. Obviously the success or failure of the Spens scheme in any school will depend on the personality of the man who is responsible for ' Scripture teaching '. To the Christian, Holy Scripture is the record of revelation ; not a summary of religious opinions held by men however eminent. From the right man, and only from the right man, will pupils learn that the Bible is at once human and divine.

The value of the Spens Report, the work of a committee, which is as one might expect somewhat tentative and fragmentary, lies chiefly in the encouragement it gives to headmasters and Education Authorities to throw baseless fears to the wind. In the Elementary school it has been conclusively proved that fears of sectarian propaganda at the hands of teachers are entirely unjustified. Experience shows that difficulty lies not so much in the temptation to stress denominational difference, as in the fact that Christians are still divided in regard to the application of Christian principles to modern life. In this respect no school can march far ahead of contemporary opinion. The tragic fact of recent years has been that parents and Church have often laid an intolerable burden on the teacher's shoulders. Only as Church and home and school co-operate can religious education be properly given. When these conditions are fulfilled and only when these conditions are fulfilled, will the teacher be free to devote himself to what is surely his proper task, that of dealing with objective historic facts in the confident hope that these when properly presented will automatically affect heart, mind and will of those committed to his care.

# BIBLIOGRAPHY

*Chapter II*

W. H. Woodward : Desiderius Erasmus concerning the aim and method of Education (Cambridge, 1904).

J. A. Froude : Short Studies of Great Subjects (1909), Vol. I, pp. 39-153, Luther and Erasmus.

J. H. Lupton : A Life of Dean Colet. Eng. Trans. of Colet's Lectures on Romans and 1st Corinthians.

*Chapter III*

F. Watson : The English Grammar Schools to 1660 (Cambridge, 1908).

A. Nowell : A Catechism written in Latin by A. Nowell . . . together with the same translated into English by T. Norton (Parker Society, 1853).

*Chapter IV*

F. Paulsen : German Education past and present. English Translation by T. Lorenz (London, 1908), pp. 79-85.

T. Hughes : Loyola and the Educational System of the Jesuits (New York, 1892).

R. Schwickerath : Jesuit Education : Its History and Principles viewed in the Light of Modern Educational Problems (St. Louis, 1904).

See also articles on Jesuits in the Catholic Encyclopaedia, Vol. 14.

Schaff-Herzog, Vol. 6 ; Monroe's Cyclopaedia of Education, Vol. 3, pp. 533-41.

Rein's Encyclopaedisches Handbuch der Pädagogik (Jesuiten-Pädagogik, Jesuiten-Schulen).

*Chapter V*

M. W. Keatinge : The Great Didactic of Comenius (A. C. Black, 1896).

S. S. Laurie : J. A. Comenius : his life and educational works (6th ed., 1899).

*Chapter VI*

Nothing of much value on Francke or Pietism is to be found in English. His story of the founding of the Orphanage (Segens-volle Fuszstapfen) was frequently translated in the eighteenth century, e.g. edited by Woodward, 1706. 'An abstract of the Marvellous Footsteps of Divine Providence.' Life of A. H. Francke, (Religious Tract Society, 1833).

A. H. Francke : Pädagogische Schriften, edited by D. G. Kramer (1885).

A. H. Francke : Zum Gedächtnis (Halle, 1927).

A. H. Francke : Ein Lebensbild, by D. G. Kramer, 2 vols. (Halle, 1880).

*Chapter VII*

H. W. MEYER : Child Nature and Nurture in Zinzendorf (New York, 1929).

O. UTTENDOERFER : Das Erziehungswesen Zinzendorfs (1912).

O. UTTENDOERFER : Zinzendorf und die Jugend (1913).

*Chapter VIII*

Pestalozzi's Educational Writings, edited by J. A. Green (1912).

How Gertrude teaches her Children. Translated by L. E. Holland and F. C. Turner, (3rd ed. 1904).

J. A. GREEN : Life and Work of Pestalozzi (1913).

G. COMPAYRE : Pestalozzi and Elementary Education (1907).

*Chapter IX*

A. R. OSBORN : Schleiermacher and Religious Education.

Selected Sermons of Schleiermacher, translated by Mary F. Wilson (1890).

Schleiermacher's Soliloquies, translated by H. L. Friess (Chicago, 1926).

Schleiermacher on Religion. Speeches . . . (Reden), translated by J. Oman (1893).

The Christian Faith (Glaubenslehre), English Translation (1928).

*Chapter X*

Sermons by Thomas Arnold (New Edition revised by his daughter, Mrs. W. E. Forster), 6 vols. (London, 1878).

STANLEY : The Life and Correspondence of Thomas Arnold.

FINDLAY (J. J.) : Arnold of Rugby, 1897.

FITCH (Sir J. G.) : Thomas and Matthew Arnold, 1897.

MACK (E. C.) : Public Schools and British Opinion, 1780-1860, pp. 236-75 (London, 1938).

*Chapter XI*

SMITH (F.) : A History of English Elementary Education (1760-1902).

HOWARD (J.) : Historical sketch of the York (C. of E.) Sunday School Committee (1887).

Report of the Consultative Committee on Secondary Education (Spens Report) (1938).

Educating for Democracy. A volume of essays, edited by J. L. Cohen and R. M. W. Travers (Macmillan, 1939).

ROSALIND MURRAY : The Good Pagan's Failure (Longmans, 1939).